979.494
S651a
1989

ALIVE IN LA LA LAND

ALIVE IN

Jack Smith

FRANKLIN WATTS
New York   Toronto
1989

Library of Congress Cataloging-in-Publication Data

To the nurses and doctors
of the USC-County Medical Center,
with thanks for bringing me back from the dead

AUTHOR'S NOTE

Most of the pieces in this book appeared first in the *Los Angeles Times*. I am grateful to that newspaper for permission to collect them here. As usual, I must thank my wife for her patience and assistance.

CONTENTS

Pilgrimage

Getting Around

Brain Damage

Hollywood Then

Disaster

Samantha

The Way We Were

The Animal World

Books, Music

Watch Your Language

The Sound of Music

How to Live Long

State of the Art

Brave New World

Word Processing

Subject A

The Great American Sport

Sex in the Movies

Improbable Conveniences

La La Land of the Novel

I Don't Like Vegetables

Doomsday

L.A. Song

PROLOGUE

Whence La La Land?

Few cities have suffered and at the same time reveled in as many epithets as Los Angeles.

We are known as the Nowhere City, Smogville, the Capital of Kitsch, Double Dubuque, Lotus Land, Moronia, the Fake Tomato Factory, Forty Suburbs in Search of a City, and Will Rogers's affectionate contribution, Cuckooland.

A relative newcomer, but very much in vogue, is La La Land.

I'm not sure of its origin. I thought I had discovered it in *Atencion San Miguel*, a small English-language newspaper published in San Miguel de Allende, in the Mexican highlands.

In writing about her recent visit to Los Angeles, Mimi Loomer said she found it shocking.

"Of course," she wrote, "when in La La Land you must see Rodeo Drive. . . ."

La La Land. It sounded as if it might be a corruption of Lotus Land, an old favorite. It seemed to symbolize the usual clichés about our laid-back life-style, our mindless, sybaritic, inarticulate, hottub, self-indulgent ways. It was derived, perhaps, from "Ooh la la!" and "Tra la la," expressions of sexual titillation and simpleminded lollygagging.

1

2

A specific origin is suggested by Daniel Fredgant of Woodland Hills:

"Stevie Wonder, in his early 1986 album 'In Square Circle,' has a song titled 'Land of La La,' and the refrain makes it clear that the song is about our fair city, with Stevie and backup singers singing spirited 'el-lays' every few beats. . . ."

Corroboration comes from Jim Robinson, Latin teacher, Madison High School, San Diego, on the highest authority —his teenage daughter.

> My 13-year-old daughter, Tarlie, who knows every word to every song written since 1983, says that Mimi Loomer has not "added an epithet to our lexicon." She claims that Stevie Wonder recorded a song called "Land of La La" at least a year ago and that the lyrics clearly allude to your fine city . . ."

I am happy to add one documented epithet to the many that have been bestowed on our city in this century.

Coincidentally, I have just rediscovered the origin of one of the oldest of Los Angeles epithets—"Double Dubuque."

I would have guessed that Double Dubuque was of theatrical origin. Obviously it was invented by some roadshow wit who had played Dubuque and considered Los Angeles the same kind of hick town but twice as big.

A letter found in a forgotten file reminds me that this durable epithet, according to H. Allen Smith in *Lost in the Horse Latitudes*, was invented by the waggish Rufus Blair, a Paramount publicist, probably in the 1930s.

It is still as full of meaning and insult as any others, including those with more venom.

In the first chapter of his book Smith writes: "Just recently I returned to New York City from Hollywood. I spent six months in the town Rufus Blair calls Double Dubuque."

Smith also tells a story about Blair ordering a glass of

brandy from a new bartender. He gagged on it, called it unfit for human consumption, and pushed it back across the bar. He ordered a whiskey instead. The bartender poured him a whiskey. He drank the whiskey and started to walk away.

The bartender said, 'You didn't pay for the whiskey."

"I traded the brandy for it," Blair said.

"But you didn't pay for the brandy," the bartender complained.

"Why should I?" Blair said. "I didn't drink it."

He walked away, leaving the bartender to puzzle it out.

Now a man capable of that is capable, I suggest, of inventing Double Dubuque. I consider my research closed.

Smith also attempts to nail down Frank Lloyd Wright's famous remark about Southern California. Smith says, "I've not been able to find it anywhere in print, but it was recited to me as follows:

"It is as though God had taken hold of the United States, at the tip of Maine, just as a person might take hold of a handkerchief. He lifted that one corner and began shaking it, and all the unstable elements in the country were shaken loose and deposited down in the opposite corner. That is Southern California."

The version I heard was simpler: "It's as if someone tilted the continent to the west and everything loose slid into Los Angeles."

To the Infinite Horizons

Literary put-downs of Los Angeles don't offend me. I cherish them. A city that inspires such contempt must have character.

Now and then, in recent years, I have imagined that the

LaLaLand

4   flow of abuse from eastern and foreign journalists and pundits was abating, but then some envious columnist, novelist, or professor of anthropology would fire a new fusillade of the same clichés, and I realized that the bait was still being taken.

"I am well aware," writes Eric Engdahl, "of the abuse heaped upon southern California and its inmates. New Yorkers, of course, led by Woody Allen, seem to have started it."

Engdahl evidently refers to Allen's remark "I don't want to live in a place where the only cultural advantage is being able to turn right on a red light."

But it started long before Woody Allen, and it was a man from Cambridge, Massachusetts, a Harvard man, Richard Henry Dana, author of *Two Years Before the Mast*, who started it. Stopping in San Pedro in 1835, Dana wrote in his diary that Los Angeles looked hazy from there, and he couldn't wait to go on to San Francisco.

The modern genre of invective was invented by a turncoat, Willard Huntington Wright, a long-ago literary editor of the *Los Angeles Times* who later wrote the Philo Vance detective novels as S. S. Van Dyne. Writing in *Smart Set* magazine back in 1913, Mr. Wright described Los Angeles as being settled by yokels from the Midwest—yokels "who were nourished by rural pieties and superstitions and had a righteous abhorrence of shapely legs, late dinners, malt liquors, grand opera and hussies."

In 1926 the so-called sage of Baltimore, Henry L. Mencken, made the obligatory trip to "the coast" and reported that "the whole place stank of orange blossoms." It was on that occasion that he dubbed our town Moronia.

A decade later curmudgeon Westbrook Pegler wrote, "It is earnestly proposed that the U.S.A. would be much better off if that big, sprawling, incoherent, shapeless, slobbering civic idiot, the city of Los Angeles, could be declared incompetent and placed in the charge of a guardian."

More recently, the Chicago columnist Mike Royko

wrote that the entire state of California should be fenced in to protect the rest of the country from its lunatics.

However, Edward Condren, professor of English at UCLA, asserts that in the field of academia, which he sees at first hand, Los Angeles is not only no longer a cultural desert; it is the promised land. He writes:

> Scarcely anyone disbelieves the accepted wisdom that Los Angeles blots the national copybook. I, too, as a native New Yorker, once dined out on that view. But after living here 18 years, and noticing that the behavior of our detractors actually contradicts what they say, I have been completely weaned away.

He admits that as a Chaucerian scholar he may have an academic's narrow picture of how he came to be fond of Los Angeles. The "first revelation," he says, was the city's obvious appeal to "touring intelligentsia."

He notes that all an eastern academic has to do to double his salary is mention an invitation from Los Angeles. "Why, in my profession dozens of careers are enhanced every year at the mere suggestion of a visit to Los Angeles, only very few of which actually concern an appointment."

He concludes, from these observations, that UCLA must be "the finest academic appointment in the world"; whatever one's criteria—"health of budget, access to ancillary careers, flora and fauna, championship athletic teams— UCLA comes out on top."

But the single most important consideration in the eastern academic's yearning for Los Angeles, Condren says, is the location and climate.

> How warm will academic reputation keep on the banks of the Charles River, never mind the chilly athletic tradition there? And in Chicago they must recruit with bound columns of Mike Royko—what other comfort is there? In Princeton I understand

6 they're trying to flunk Brookie (Brooke Shields) to keep their lone enticement around . . .

Steve Grant of Thousand Oaks also writes to express his impatience with critics of Los Angeles.

Did anyone really ask them? Who cares if they like it? What did they expect, anyway? Instant friends waiting to welcome them with open arms? Wood nymphs frolicking midst sylvan glades?

And while we're on the subject, is a ticky-tacky tract home in the sunshine really worse than a sturdy tenement (excuse me—brownstone) built to last 100 years (and in its 97th) where the skies are cloudy all day?

I would just like to add that it would be a mistake to think that we don't have wood nymphs frolicking midst sylvan glades.

Meanwhile, another newcomer to Los Angeles has a different vision of it. Adeline Bingham, instructor in basic skills and English as a second language at Coastline Community College, sends me the following paragraph written by one of her immigrant students:

"Driving my car on the freeway at night makes me having my best delightful . . . It's to enjoy the two light streams, one is red and another is white. They flow stoplessly in the opposition directions to the infinitive horizon."

All you have to do to be a poet is feel the wonder of living in Los Angeles.

Fiat Lux

More and more visitors seem to find Los Angeles exciting, beautiful, adventurous, surprising, exotic, and free. Even livable.

I have called Los Angeles the freest city in the world; now Tom Shales of the *Washington Post,* a distinguished eastern newspaper, comes along to add a word:

Writing about the faith that underlies the television industry here, he said: "That's one of the reasons I love coming to Los Angeles and to Hollywood. People here still believe. The sun comes out every day and smacks them in the face and they march off gamely to face insurmountable odds. Los Angeles may be the most renewable city in the world. . . ."

There you have it. Free and renewable. Of what other great city can those two words be said?

Shales also discovered something I have always known about Los Angeles.

"People who want to complain about Los Angeles say they miss the change of seasons. I think there's really more changing of seasons here, not less. Every Monday morning, you wake up, and you look outside, and it's spring again. . . ."

No visitors seem to appreciate us more than the Australians. Leonie Sandercock, a professor of urban studies at Macquarie University, recently returned to Australia after living and teaching here for six months. She wrote of Los Angeles in the *Sydney Morning Herald* with rare insight and understanding.

"I happen to think that Sydney is just about the most physically exhilarating and sensual city in the world . . ." she said.

I have been captivated by the hazy Tuscan light on cypress hills, the colours of the buildings along Venetian canals, the angles of terracotta roofs in Flor-

8 ence . . . What I never expected was to be drawn, physically, to L.A.

Yet, to my astonishment, I became attached to the view from the freeway of the palm trees floating and receding down empty avenues; attached to the deceptive perspectives of the pale subtropical light; to the backdrop of the Hollywood Hills, so much like a movie set; to the scurrying sandpipers and saluting seagulls on Santa Monica Beach at sunrise; to the view of the Milky Way and its shooting stars that you get at 3 A.M. after a two hour drive to the Mojave Desert; to drinks in the long summer evenings in the Hollywood Hills overlooking the city as it turns on its fairy lights; and even to Sunset Strip itself, that raucous celebration of popular culture . . .

Pamela Fiori, editor of *Travel & Leisure* magazine, said simply in a recent issue on Los Angeles,

Los Angeles is like no other place in America; at the same time, it seems more American than anyplace else. . . . Right now L.A. is at its best. . . . It isn't even flaky anymore (well . . . maybe just a tad). And I haven't heard anyone use the word 'laid back' in years. . . .

Fiori also quoted an observation by another Australian, Clive James:

"The awkward truth about L.A. is that although it dares you to laugh at it, you can't. No free person can afford to mock Los Angeles, since liberty is its primary impulse. . . ."

Fiori adds: "Life, liberty and the pursuit of pleasure—these are the driving forces of L.A."

I'm not sure, though, that Fiori is right when she says that we are no longer 'laid back' and that, in fact, the expression has gone out of use.

Consider a letter from Jere Stuart French, a Claremont
landscape architect.

On Foothill Boulevard, near where I live, an oriental
massage, video rental, yogurt shop and a palmistry
parlor all huddle nearby, apparently accepting one
another with equanimity. I have to be reminded by
touring relations that this just isn't the way it is in
Iowa. Are we jaded or just laid back?

And as for license plates, on my way to school
one morning a sports car, probably a Z, weaved past
me on the San Berdoo Freeway, dashing into and
out of my lane and causing all us drivers in the vicin-
ity to hit the brakes. As the car shot past me on the
right I caught a glimpse of the driver—the window
being down—a resolute smile on her face, long
brown hair billowing, and forgave her. On her rapidly disappearing vanity plate I read, SCUZA ME.

Moments later I pulled off onto the Cal Poly
campus, and as I eased into the 25 m.p.h. tree-lined
drive, a bright yellow VW bug suddenly leapt into
my path from between parked cars, again requiring
evasive action on my part, standing on the brake
and hoping not to be rear-ended. Then a hundred
yards or so later she just as suddenly dove head first
into a gap too small for proper parking, leaving her
rear sticking well out into the drive lane (more evasive maneuvering). This time the driver was blond
with perky short hair, and I forgave her too. Her
license? DO I BUG U . . .

Not long ago I told my wife that my fondest wish was to
have license plates reading FIAT LUX, which means, in
Latin, "Let there be light." She told me later she had tried
to get those plates for my birthday but found out they were
already taken. I was crushed.

What I wonder about, of course, since we live in this

10   place of dreams realized and pleasure uninhibited, is whether she'd have bought me a Fiat to go with them.

Yea, L.A.

John Updike, the distinguished poet, novelist, and short-story writer, has written the last thing I would ever have expected to see from his pen—a poem about Los Angeles.

Updike lives in Ipswich, Massachusetts, and I had no idea that he'd ever been to Los Angeles, but his poem in a recent issue of *The New Yorker* was evidently inspired by a firsthand look at downtown L.A., old and new.

The poem was clipped and sent to me by Michael McNamara, of Rancho Palos Verdes, with this brief comment: "I thought you might be interested in this recent slur on Los Angeles. . . . It seems to be a bit overdone."

I quote McNamara as a courtesy, because he sent me the poem; I'm not saying I agree with him.

It is a treat to have Updike's gilded mirror held up to our city, which is so routinely maligned by less elegant journalists and jet-set novelists, and I would like to reprint his poem here in full. However, I'm sure *The New Yorker* is vigilant against infringement of its copyright, and Updike, like any other professional writer, must be the same.

Even if I were to quote only two lines, say, that would be close to 15 percent of the entire poem, which is more, I suspect, than one is permitted under copyright law for purposes of review.

Besides, I have no intention of reviewing Updike's work. I am not a literary critic, and I am quite unsophisticated about contemporary poetry. But I have always treasured the obloquies Los Angeles provokes from sensitive visitors; I collect them, and I like to pass them on to my fellow Angelenos. That we are the cause of such dyspepsia among the literati of the eastern seaboard is one of the joys of living here.

Perhaps I can reflect Updike's vision of downtown Los Angeles, if only imperfectly, by scrupulous quotation, direct and indirect, even though I know the thing is poetry and that its essence can not be captured by decanting a few phrases.

With poetic simplicity the poem is called "L.A."
It begins with the word "Yea."

The poet places himself at the top of a "paved and windy hill," which, from other clues, I take to be Bunker Hill. He is standing in weeds taller than a man, and below him, deep as a canyon, a freeway thunders.

All around him new buildings are being "assembled," as he says, by "darkish people." (I quote "darkish people" because I don't know whether Updike means sunburned people or what. To a New Englander in winter, I imagine, all of us out here look darkish.)

There is a line about Harold Lloyd "teetering" on "tan-bricked business blocks"—a nostalgic reference to that unforgettable scene from the 1930 movie *Feet First* in which Lloyd is clinging desperately to the cornice of one of those old ten-story beaux-arts office buildings on S. Spring Street.

Updike observes, however, that these buildings now "crouch low, in shade, turned slum." They crouch in shade, I suppose, because they are in the shadow of our new financial towers, which the poet sees "in all-mirror styles of blankness." (He shows an eagle's eye for decay when he notes that Spring Street has turned slum; that's hard to see from the nearest grassy hilltop.)

I had trouble for a moment with Updike's reference to a "lone pedestrian," as if he could see only one person on the downtown streets. That might have been true at night, but if the slums were in shade, then it must have been daylight; and in daylight those shadowed streets are teeming.

But maybe the lone pedestrian is poetic license; a poet would have to be a slouch to write a whole poem without using poetic license. Or maybe the lone pedestrian is sym-

LaLaLanD

12   bolic. Now that Ogden Nash is gone I hardly ever understand *The New Yorker*'s poems, especially when they don't rhyme.

Or maybe Updike was here on a Sunday. On a Sunday you might very well look down on Spring Street and see nothing but a lone pedestrian—staggering, probably, unless it happened to be an evangelist or a policeman.

In the next line, in a striking simile, Updike describes the palms as "isolate, like psychopaths." Then he sees "Conquistadorial fevers" reminiscing in the smog, which he describes as an "adobe band." Good writing. On our worst days the smog does have the color of adobe.

I don't know exactly what Updike means by Conquistadorial fevers, though, and how they happen to be reminiscing in the smog, but I'm sure this reflects the limitations of my own imagination, not his.

In his two-line windup, he notes that there is blue in the sky, too, and that it was the promise of this blue that lured "too many" people to Los Angeles—"to this waste of angels, of ever-widening gaps."

I am baffled by those "ever-widening gaps." Evidently that phrase is the nut of Updike's message, though, since it comes at the end. What can it mean? Gaps between the expectation and the reality? But that's what they all say about Los Angeles.

Of course this isn't fair. What I've done is like taking a car apart and laying out all its parts on the floor and saying, "That's a Toyota."

Updike's "L.A." is not a scattering of phrases. It's a sonnet. Get *The New Yorker* and read it yourself; maybe you can narrow the gap.

Most Unique in La La Land

I have received a flyer from a valet parking service that calls itself "the ultimate parking service," and "the Southland's most unique. . . ."

It is a lost cause to argue that *unique* means unduplicated—quite different from anything else in the world—and can not be modified by any such adjective as *most.* There are no degrees of uniqueness, except in American advertising. Everything is more unique than everything else.

So that isn't what bothers me about this flyer. It's the second paragraph:

"Valet parking is no longer a luxury for home entertaining. It has become an expected and welcome service, as it sets the tone of the party and sends the guests away at the end of the evening feeling very special and nurtured. . . ."

That seems to me an enlightening comment on the state of the social scene in Southern California.

One dare not throw a party anymore without valet parking. It is not only welcomed but expected. The implication is that if you *don't* have valet parking nobody will ever come to one of your parties again.

But the most provocative idea is that your guests, at the end of the evening, when the valet brings them their car and they drive off, will feel *nurtured.*

You used to feel lucky if they left feeling well fed and halfway sober. Now you have to feel that they feel *nurtured.*

Nurtured never appeared in print ten or fifteen years ago except in the sense of nutrition, but it is one of that bag of words that now are part of the arsenal of everyone who writes about interpersonal problems. (Nobody ever used the word *interpersonal* fifteen years ago, either.)

Now we must all have nurturing interpersonal experiences. Nurturing in that sense means supportive. *Supportive* also was never used fifteen years ago except in reference to jockstraps, brassieres, or flying buttresses—something that actually gave physical support.

14   It used to be, too, that one used the word *experience* only in reference to some exciting adventure, like losing one's virginity or being mugged in a supermarket parking lot.

Now one can have a unique shopping experience. A unique driving experience. One doesn't see a movie. One experiences it.

Well, I can see that having one's car delivered by a valet after a party might be a unique, nurturing, and supportive experience. In the past it would have been merely a convenience.

We have a whole new language, which gives some people the illusion, I suppose, that we have a whole new range of experiences. We no longer simply know people or are acquainted with people or sleep with people or are married to people; we have *relationships* with people. If two people are giving anything of themselves to each other, they are said to be making *commitments;* and if they do this for any length of time, they are said to be having an *ongoing* relationship.

If it is ongoing long enough and the commitments are deep enough, they are said to be having a *meaningful* relationship.

If any children result from such a relationship, the partners to it go into a phase called *parenting,* and if they are conscientious and supportive, they are known as *caring.*

With no connections or responsibilities to any other person it is possible to be known as a *caring* person just by feigning a caring manner when someone else is in a jam. How often we hear it said, "He's a very caring person," of some curmudgeon who has neither wife nor dog.

R. D. Rosen put his finger on this new vocabulary of phony analysis a few years ago and gave it a name in his book *Psychobabble: Fast Talk and Quick Cure in the Era of Feeling.*

Whether it is the residue of Freud, the psychological shock of World War II and the Cold War, or whatever, everyone in the Western industrial countries seemed to go in for self-psychoanalysis in the 1970s. There was a lot of easy talk about getting their heads together and getting in touch with themselves, and the result has been a rise in the divorce and crime rates and punk rock music.

Human nature hasn't changed much since Chaucer and Shakespeare, and while our institutions have changed greatly, we are just beginning to deal with the fact that men beat their wives and adults abuse children and ongoing relationships are no more meaningful than ever.

Rosen exposed the hollow language and dubious results of such fads as rebirthing, primal therapy, assertiveness training, transactional analysis, and est. The search for that "whole person" that lies within us goes on, mostly through the parlor games we play.

But it seems to me we are now about to leave the era of self-help, which has made millionaires out of dozens of hack writers of books on how to get rich, how to parent, how to achieve orgasm, how to climb the corporate ladder, and how to slide into the computer age; now we are likely to believe that everything we need to know can be purchased on a floppy disk. (We must not forget that computers can only tell us what we already know or are capable of figuring out. Garbage in, garbage out.)

Meanwhile, we should take comfort in knowing that we can be nurtured by a parking service.

Its attendants, this service advertises, are "selected individually for their efficiency, courteousness, pleasant out-going manner and their all-American look . . . and present a youthful and exuberant appearance. . . ."

They sound almost unique.

CATASTROPHE

I Had to Follow Steve Allen

At first I wasn't alarmed. I was merely puzzled. It wasn't a pain in my chest. A pain in the chest was angina. The classic symptom of heart trouble.

It was more of an ache. It was in my back and shoulders. It came and went. It was just a low-grade ache, not especially painful. It was like the ache you get when you have thrown a ball too hard or made an awkward reach backward. In a moment it would go away.

Then I began to notice other symptoms. Sometimes the ache would be accompanied by a feeling of fatigue. Sometimes I perspired and felt faint.

I began to associate the trouble with certain activities, looking for some telltale relationship. I noticed that the ache often came when I was under stress.

I was often under stress at that time. I was not only writing five columns a week for the *Los Angeles Times* but also making talks around Southern California to library support groups, to journalism groups, and simply here and there, whenever I was called on.

One night when I was to make a talk before the Friends of the La Verne Library, my wife and I had dinner earlier at the home of one of the friends. It was warm and pleasant, and I enjoyed the company and the meal.

17

18   We drove to the university, where I was to talk at
Founders Hall. We parked the car across the street and got
out. It was rather chilly for Southern California. As we
walked across the street, I began to feel faint. Once inside
the hall, I said, "I think I'd better sit down for a minute."

I sat in a wooden chair in the entrance hall. My shoulders began to ache. Perspiration broke out on my forehead.
I trembled. I wondered whether I was having a heart attack
and what I should do.

Suddenly the symptoms went away. Strength flowed
back into me. I was all right. Whatever it was, it wasn't
important.

I got up and went into the auditorium and talked the
usual forty-five minutes.

A week or two later I attended an awards ceremony in
Hollywood. I was receiving an award from some Hollywood
women's advertising group on one pretext or another. So
was Steve Allen. For some inexplicable reason Allen was
called on to speak before I was.

I sat there at my table realizing that I was going to have
to follow Steve Allen. It was not an enviable position. I felt
a streak of pain in my upper arms and across my shoulders.
I began to perspire. I felt faint.

Whatever it was, then, it was definitely associated with
stress.

I decided it was time to tell my doctor about it. I described the symptoms and the circumstances in which they
appeared.

He shook his head skeptically. "I doubt if it's got anything to do with your heart," he said. "There's just nothing
in your history to indicate heart trouble."

It was true. By outward appearance I did not look like a
prime prospect for a heart attack. I was sixty-seven years
old, but I had always been thin. My blood pressure was
under control. I wasn't a weekend athlete. I didn't exert
myself. I didn't smoke.

Actually, I hadn't worried much about my heart. In his
classic book *Type A Behavior and Your Heart*, Dr. Meyer

Friedman's first paragraph had been a quotation from my column in the *Times*:

"Some time ago," I had written, "I quit worrying about what to do, or not to do, to keep from having a heart attack. I was so confused by all the conflicting theories that I began developing the symptoms."

My doctor told me to let him know if my pain recurred.

I Flunked the Angiogram

A week or so later I was walking up a ramp with my wife to buy tickets for a trip to Catalina when the pain came suddenly and hard. It was deep and lasting. I had to sit down until it went away.

I went back to my doctor. That was enough for him.

"We'll have to give you a stress test," he said.

He made an appointment for me at Huntington Memorial Hospital, and I went in for my stress test. A stress test consists mainly of walking on a treadmill at a gradually increasing speed and degree of incline. Meanwhile, your blood pressure and your heart rate are monitored.

After three minutes I was unable to go on.

I had flunked the test.

My doctor said it was time to consult a cardiologist.

The cardiologist was a pleasant, polite, low-key southern gentleman who seemed unflappable. He said I would have to have an angiogram.

The angiogram is a supposedly simple procedure in which a plastic catheter is inserted into an artery in the thigh, threaded through the body and into the aorta itself. Dyes are passed through the catheter and photographed by X ray. If the blood vessels that send blood to the heart are blocked by fatty tissues, as in atherosclerosis, the flow of dye is shut off or squeezed down to a trickle.

One must stay in the hospital overnight for an angiogram. It is, I have since learned, a rather hazardous proce-

20   dure. But it is not entirely unpleasant. One is lightly drugged, and one can lie back and watch the dye enter one's heart on a screen.

I flunked the angiogram, too.

"What does that mean?" I asked my cardiologist.

He said it meant surgery. I would have to have a coronary bypass.

Bypass is medical vernacular for coronary artery bypass graft surgery—in which the surgeon takes a length of vein from one's leg and grafts it from the aorta to the heart, bypassing a blocked coronary artery.

It was merely a phrase to me. Some of my friends had had them. They all swore it was a piece of cake. They felt better afterward than they had in ten years.

The operation has become so commonplace as to seem trivial, but it is still a major operation.

My cardiologist called in the surgeon, who of course corroborated his finding.

I didn't argue. I didn't demand a second opinion. I believed I was in good hands.

"When do you want to do it?" I asked.

"Tuesday," the surgeon said.

That was Friday.

Would It Make Any Difference?

No matter how routine heart surgery has become, there is always a chance that the patient will die.

I didn't give a lot of thought to it. I had committed my share of sins in my life; I would like to have been able to undo them—at least some of them; but when the bell tolls, you don't get a second chance.

Or do you?

I had faced death at least once before. I had landed in the third wave with the marines on Iwo Jima, an island

whose name, sad to say, means nothing to the youth of
today.

The Japanese were shelling the beach ferociously. At
the time our amtrac landed, casualties were running 75 percent. The chances for survival were not good. I ran up the
beach and stumbled down into a shell hole made either by a
Japanese field piece or by our own preparatory naval gunfire. Two other men clambered into the hole behind me. We
could hardly talk above the din.

We looked at each other dumbly. Fear was the common
denominator. I suggested that we should get out of the hole,
because if we stayed there it would soon take another hit.
The Japanese were zeroed in on that beach.

"We have to get off the beach and go on forward," I
argued. I was a sergeant, but not a line sergeant. I had no
authority over those marines. I have often wondered since
whether they saw the number 3 on the back of my blouse,
for sergeant, and deferred to my rank.

They agreed, and the two of them climbed up to the lip
of the hole and flung themselves forward, over the top. I
was right behind them. Just as my head reached the top of
the hole, a shell landed a few feet forward of it. My helmet
rang as if hit by a sledgehammer. I was stunned. When my
head cleared, I climbed on up and out of the hole.

One of my comrades had vanished. The other was in a
kneeling position, as if praying. He had no head.

Besides carrying a lifelong load of guilt over that inci-
dent, I have always wondered why I was spared.

I thought of myself as having had a second chance.

Now, with most of my life spent and few of my sins
expiated, I was about to have heart surgery, and if I was
lucky, I would have yet another chance.

If I survived, would it make any difference in my life?
Would I live more fully? Would I be more generous, kind,
loving?

I checked into the hospital on Tuesday, and on Wednes-
day morning they wheeled me into surgery. I was so

22 drugged that philosophical introspections were beyond me. Deep down, I knew that I might never wake up, but it didn't really trouble me.

I was in surgery four and a half hours. My surgeon did four bypasses, not one; on the table I suffered a minor heart attack, and one of the bypasses did not work.

I am not going to describe the operation step by step. I never asked about it, for one thing. Also, I don't share the common notion that everyone is interested in everyone else's operation.

Looking back, I'm sure that the most disturbing part of the entire experience was my loss of mental stability during my recovery.

I am increasingly aware of my faults and weaknesses, but until then I was satisfied that in a mad world I was relatively sane. In every crisis, no matter how poorly I may have acted out of character deficiency, I at least knew what was what.

I Was Being Held Against My Will

From the time I woke up in the intensive care unit until I was wheeled into a room of my own, with windows, flowers, and television, I imagined I was a prisoner. I never had any idea what they wanted with me. I was neither rich enough for ransom nor young and seductive enough for sexual exploitation. Perhaps, it occurred to me in one of my darkest moments, they wanted my body for scientific uses.

I don't understand the physiology and psychology of it, but I will guess that this fantasy took root somehow during my deep anesthesia, when they had stopped my heart and I was running on a blood circulating machine. For four and a half hours my brain was dependent on that machine for its nourishment.

In the postoperative womb of intensive care, during the hours when I was gradually swimming up from the deeps of unconsciousness, I began to write on my computer. Endlessly. Pouring out pages of exposition so articulate, so balanced, so illuminating, that I knew I could never repeat them. I was afire with the creative process. I don't know how long I wrote, or what about. It seemed days.

It was urgent, I knew, that those words must be preserved, must reach the outside world.

Finally, I realized I was conscious, therefore alive, in a quiet, windowless room. The only sound was a metronomic little ping. Ominous. Not ominous because it didn't stop, I sensed, but because it might. It was my heart, beating in a monitor.

A nurse hovered. An orderly appeared. Heavyset. Strong bare arms. Actually, if he was there to restrain me, he was overqualified.

I am not going to tell you all about the ICU. For one thing, I don't remember. Most of the time, I was under.

I believed I was being held against my will when I woke up and found my wrists and ankles tied to the bed. I was breathing through a plastic tube that had been slid through my nose and down through my windpipe into the lung. Because of it I couldn't talk.

Panic: I cannot stand to be restrained. In movies, I empathize with the badman who snarls, "You'll never get me behind bars."

Not being able to talk, of course, was the worst part of it. I couldn't even complain.

I gestured frantically with my hands, demanding an explanation. The nurse was rather small, with dark hair and eyes. She looked stern. She reminded me of one of the Borgias. (Later, of course, she turned out to be an angel, like all the others.) She explained.

I had complained. That was the problem. During the night I had ripped out the oxygen tube. They had had to have me reanesthetized to put the tube back in, and then they had tied me to keep me from tearing it out again.

24   That night my older son came. He stood at the foot of the bed, saying he wished he could help me. I wiggled my fingers, indicating he could set me free.

He said he couldn't do it. They wouldn't let him.

That's when I realized that he was in their power, too. What had they used? Drugs? Some terrible threat? Where was my wife?

When I next awoke, my doctor was looking down at me. Not my surgeon, not my cardiologist, not any of the hospital doctors. My own doctor. My friend. He wore a gray business suit. He had an aura of the outside world, fresh and free.

Thank God. He had come to save me.

I wiggled my fingers and croaked my outrage. Patiently he explained why they had had to tie me.

Whatever the emotion is that lies below despair, I struck it.

There was no hope. They had him, too.

That night I wrote millions of words on my computer, crying out to posterity.

COMEBACK

She Was the Bartender at the Folies-Bergère

In that half-life between anesthesia and wakefulness, as I lay in the dim intensive care unit, I became obsessed by the millions of words I imagined I was turning out by computer. It was my lifework. It would expose the tyranny of the world—especially the medical world.

I did not seem to be able to relate this process of creation to the fact that my computer sat on its desk in my den ten miles away, disconnected, idle, and mute.

The fantasy stayed with me until I had been graduated from intensive care into my own room, with a window looking out on trees and sky, and was floating back toward sanity.

Let me say that I believe Huntington Memorial is a benign institution, efficiently run, with amiable and competent people, including my doctors and nurses, every one, and the nameless troops—there seemed to be dozens of them—who came in cheerfully every hour or so to take my blood. I was not, of course, the victim of a conspiracy and kidnapping. I was simply the victim of an already febrile mind emerging from deep anesthesia and the shock of a quadruple bypass operation.

The hospital is beautifully situated in old Pasadena above the arroyo and below the mountains. Except that my

26 mind seems to run along darker channels, I might have imagined, in recovery, that I was staying at the nearby Huntington-Sheraton Hotel.

I was nevertheless convinced, for days, that I was in sinister hands, abandoned not only by my own doctor and my family but by the human race. As for my belief that I was writing everything down on my computer so the world would know, that was perhaps no more than a more intense case of the anxiety nightmares I often have about my work.

But its profound depth and persistence were revealed to me one evening when I was in recovery, and theoretically quite rational, and was visited by my younger son. He is very good with computers, so I actually asked him:

"Do you think there is any way that I could be writing anything here and getting it out over my computer?" (When I am at home and the computer is working, I can send my copy over the telephone to the *Times.)*

He looked at me with what must have been alarm and dismay. He shook his head slowly. "I don't see how," he said. He didn't laugh.

I was relieved. I had begun to realize that everything I had composed in my delirium was junk.

Somehow, being reassured about the computer file, I began to see that the whole idea of a conspiracy had been a phantom. At that discovery I took a big step back toward sanity.

Even so, the line between illusion and reality remained blurred. My night dreams were vivid, and when the day nurse made her first call—I was usually already awake—I would try to find out from her, with oblique questions, whether what I had dreamed was true.

"You've been dreaming," she sometimes said. Or, "No, I don't think so," not laughing.

It is a cherished myth that men invariably fall in love with their nurses. I didn't do that; but I felt close enough to most of them to see that it really must happen.

One of them, near the end of my stay, looked hauntingly familiar. I knew that face: fair, pleasant, reflective, modestly voluptuous. Suddenly it came to me. She was the girl in the French Impressionist painting—the bartender at the Folies-Bergère. The likeness enchanted me. I loved to watch her moving about the room at her chores—all those lovely womanly movements. I wondered whether Degas had ever painted or sculpted nurses.

"You know who that nurse looks like?" I asked my wife one day.

She said the young woman did look familiar, but she couldn't place her.

I said, "The bartender at the Folies-Bergère. In Manet's painting.

"You're right," she said. "But wasn't it Toulouse-Lautrec? And wasn't it the Moulin Rouge? Not the Folies-Bergère?"

"No," I said. "I'm sure of it. It was Manet. And it was the Folies-Bergère."

I asked her to look it up in our Manet book when she got home. "There's a full-page reproduction of it," I said, "and also a detail showing just the girl's head and shoulders."

She said, "I still think it was Toulouse-Lautrec."

"Bring the book," I said. "I want to show her."

The next day she brought the book. "You were right," she said. "It was Manet, and the Folies-Bergère."

I showed the picture to the nurse. She was entranced, like some wood nymph seeing her reflection for the first time in a pool.

I was a long way from whole; but that little triumph brought me back into the light.

My memory had proved true; I had remembered that a certain picture had been painted by Manet, not Toulouse-Lautrec. An exquisite point, it seemed to me. And I had introduced a young woman to *Le Bar des Folies-Bergère.*

28

We Love You, Mr. Smith

Something unexpected and wonderful waited for us the day my wife drove me up the hill to our house after my two weeks in the hospital.

Our house is on the corner of the top of a steep rise, so that you come upon it suddenly. My surprise was complete.

It was a white paper poster—two feet high and fourteen feet long—with this message blocked in across it in green crayon:

WELCOME HOME

WE LOVE YOU, MR. SMITH

It was supported by two poles planted among my wife's African daisies, and no one who drove up the hill could miss it.

Up close we saw that it was signed by Eric and Sarah and April and Elaine and Tanya and Gabriel and Karen and Michael and Amy and Nicole and Robert and Christopher and Carlos and dozens of other children who go to the little Mount Washington School at the top of the hill.

Our own boys had gone through it, and my wife had been president of the PTA. It has always had an exuberant spirit, and I have often gone up for a visit, in recent years, just to cheer myself up and restore my faith in schools, teachers, and children. Now they had brought their cheer to me.

I tottered up the steps to our door on my wife's arm and stood there gasping, reminded painfully of my devastating weakness. At the same time I was laughing. The poster had made me laugh, because men don't cry.

My cardiologist, who speaks with a gentle southern inflection that seems to make even bad news sound rather pleasant, had warned me that patients were often depressed after heart surgery.

"Why is that?" I asked. I may be disenchanted, but I remain buoyant, and I have always thought of depression as something ridiculous that you simply get, like gallstones.

The patient is depressed, the doctor told me, because he is obliged to contemplate his own mortality. I assured him that the certainty of mortality was an old acquaintance of mine and I would have no trouble with it.

I was depressed for weeks. But I don't think my heart was as much the cause of it as my nose. Evidently in yanking out my oxygen tube in the intensive care unit I had damaged the mucous membrane and had come home with a stubborn infection that filled my nose with crust, blocking the passages and making it hard or impossible for me to breathe in a normal way. The usual remedies failed or made it worse; finally, I went to an ear, nose, and throat man who gave me temporary relief by cleaning out my nose with tweezers, made laboratory tests of the infection, and prescribed a penicillin drug that eventually made me well.

I don't want to depress the reader with tedious medical details, but I describe this affliction to help explain, perhaps, my curious mental incapacity during this period.

As many patients secretly do, I suspect, I had looked forward to my convalescence. There would be a time, I imagined, when I would be over the shock and pain and before I was fit enough to go back to work, when the days would seem idyllic. Only lightly drugged, excused from every responsibility, I could read, watch TV, putter about, write thank-you notes, gradually begin to reconnect, every now and then reminding myself, I don't *have* to do anything.

I enjoyed no such interlude. The combination of physical frailty and difficulty in breathing kept me in a state of unrelieved anxiety. I couldn't concentrate. I kept trying things and bumping into my limits. I couldn't sleep. Every time I was about to drop off I remembered that I couldn't breathe through my nose. I worried that I would be asphyxiated.

I watched television night and day. Ordinarily I like

stories of crime, detection, and suspense, but the ones I tuned in were too complicated or too harrowing. I found I couldn't stand to watch anyone being handcuffed or bound or gagged or choked. Also I couldn't follow the plots.

Then one day I happened on a series I had never watched before. It was about two youths who rescue a girl from modern pirates in the Caribbean. It was great. I don't remember what the series was called, but it was based on the old Hardy Boys books for juveniles.

I had regressed that far.

I tried to watch the Dodgers, but sometimes they weren't on TV, and when they were, they were usually playing so badly I almost wished they weren't being televised.

I read, but I couldn't stay with anything but detective novels filled with sex and violence—and they had to be old ones that I had already read so that I didn't have to work too hard at the plots and didn't get too anxious over the suspense.

I put the Sunday crossword puzzle on the dining table and pecked away at it at breakfast and lunch; but I found that whenever I didn't immediately think of the required word I couldn't stand the frustration, the sense of being trapped in a maze.

Finally, one morning in the last week of school, I got a letterhead and a pen and laboriously wrote a note to the teachers and children of Mount Washington School, thanking them; it was short and not very eloquent, but I did it.

My wife drove it up to the school and gave it to the principal, who said it was just in time. There was to be an assembly in five minutes, and she would read it.

So the children of Mount Washington School were not only the first to welcome me home; they were also the first to get me back into circulation.

PILGRIMAGE

In Search of Her Roots

While I waited for time to restore my brain and body, my wife, Denise, I knew, was driving across France in a rented Renault, taking her older brother and sister on a long-postponed mission.

They were going to Lees-Athas.

Lees-Athas, which few Americans can ever have heard of, is a village in the Pyrenees a few kilometers below the French-Spanish border; it is the village in which my wife's mother was born and from which, at twenty, she had set out alone, nearly seventy-five years earlier, to emigrate to America as an indentured domestic.

My wife had made her pilgrimage to Lees-Athas only a year before, with me at the wheel of the Renault. We had swung through a great detour to take in the countryside of Burgundy, the museum cities of northern Italy, and the voluptuous resorts of the Riviera, but our true goal was Lees-Athas—if indeed such a place still existed.

My wife was in search of her roots. She knew that her mother had left younger brothers and sisters behind, but she had never heard from any of them; she didn't even know their names, and she had no idea whether any of them were still alive. She hoped, at least, to find some cousins.

Except for the first two nights in Paris, we traveled

32 without hotel reservations and without any fixed itinerary. By the time we had seen Dijon, Geneva, Verona, Venice, Milan, and the Riviera, we had only two days left before we must return to Paris to catch our plane.

Our starting point was to be the town of Pau, in the province of Pyrénées-Atlantique, southwestern France, at the base of the Pyrenees. We stayed at a pleasant little motel in the woods near Tarbes, then drove into Pau the next morning.

My wife's chances of success seemed slight. All she knew was that her mother, Suzanne Casenave, the oldest in a family of four boys and three girls, had been born in a village in the Pyrenees above Pau, not far from the Spanish border, and had lived there until the age of twenty.

She had worked out her bond in San Francisco, then gone to the small mountain town of Tehachapi, in Southern California, where a relative had found employment for her in a boardinghouse. One of the boarders was Ernest Bresson, a handsome sheepherder of her age. He had come from the French Alps, she from the Pyrenees; they met and married in the Tehachapis.

In time they moved down into the San Joaquin Valley and settled in Bakersfield, where they raised three children. My wife's mother died in 1948, her father ten years later. My wife's legacy was the stories her mother had told of her childhood in the village. There were no letters, no documents, nothing but a yellowed snapshot of an uncle—her mother's youngest brother—in the uniform of a gendarme.

It wasn't until her own children were grown that my wife began to think about her origins, but the idea of finding her mother's village was only an improbable dream. She had never been to France and had small hope of going. Then, in 1970, our younger son was married to a Frenchwoman in Tours, and of course she had to be there. Before the wedding she and our son and his fiancée set out in a rented car to search for the roots that were not only hers but also his.

They drove to Gap, in the Alps, hoping to set out from there for her father's village, but it was winter, and they were discouraged from trying the roads. Without much hope but still determined, they drove south and west to Pau. She couldn't even remember the name of her mother's village. She thought that if she saw it on a map she might recognize it. They found the tourist bureau and studied the local maps, but no bell rang.

She wanted to push on into the mountains toward the Spanish border. By then, feeling herself close to her goal, she was driven like Ronald Colman in his search for Shangri-La; but time was running out; the weather was bitter cold, and they were told that the road to Spain was deep in snow. She gave up.

Now, thirteen years later, she was back. Her sister in Bakersfield had found out from relatives in San Francisco that the name of the village was Lees-Athas; but we hadn't found it on our maps.

"It probably doesn't even exist anymore," she said, not daring to hope too much.

"Villages don't just disappear," I said; but I wondered if any of her aunts and uncles would be alive.

"Maybe there'll be some cousins," she said, still hoping.

In Pau that morning I drove cautiously down the busy rue du Marechal Foch, still hating French traffic. Then, incredibly, I saw an empty parking space. I had no idea where we were, but my rule in France was that if you saw a parking place you took it.

We parked and set out to find the tourist bureau. She asked a gendarme on a corner. He gave her directions, complete with stylish gestures and a small salute. We lost our way. She asked another gendarme. He, too, was polite and precise and saluted smartly. This time we succeeded.

It was the usual tourist bureau, with travel posters and a counter behind which two women sat. We were the only visitors. I sat down while my wife approached the counter. I had gotten her here. Now it was up to her.

One of the women was on the telephone. My wife approached the other. She started to tell her story. Suddenly the woman's face brightened, and she pointed to the woman

who was on the phone. I sensed that there had been a breakthrough.

The woman on the phone hung up. Her colleague, still glowing, spoke briefly to her. The other woman turned to my wife. They talked excitedly.

The woman picked up the phone again and dialed. She talked into the phone, now and then smiling at my wife. She took notes. She hung up and handed my wife a slip of paper, explaining the notes.

My wife thanked her exuberantly and walked unsteadily toward me. Her eyes looked out of focus. She seemed hardly to be breathing.

"I can't believe it!" she said. "She was born and raised in my mother's village!"

The woman's father had been the schoolteacher. He still lived in the village. She had telephoned him, and he had told her that two of Suzanne Casenave's brothers were still alive. One of them, Joseph, lived only a few steps from his own door.

There was a tremor in the hand that held the slip of paper.

"What do you have there?" I asked, hoping to get her back on the ground.

She looked at the note as if not believing it, either.

"It's my Uncle Ignace," she said, pronouncing it Eynya-suh. "He lives right here in Pau. It's his phone number."

"You remember his name?"

"Yes, as soon as I heard it. He was the gendarme."

It was going to be a memorable day.

"C'est Rouge! C'est Rouge!"

We spent the night in the home of my wife's uncle Ignace, her mother's youngest brother. In the morning he rode in the backseat until we were on the road to the village. He said he would walk the two or three miles home. He had spent his career as a gendarme walking, and now, at eighty, he still enjoyed it.

Until the day before, my wife had not known that her uncle Ignace was still alive or whether Lees-Athas existed. The meeting between my wife and Uncle Ignace had been emotional and gratifying. I had been afraid he might be in his dotage and not clear in his mind about who this woman from America might be. After all, he had been only seven years old when her mother left home.

When my wife telephoned, his wife answered. Monsieur Casenave was out for a walk, and Madame had to be assured that my wife wasn't some kind of swindler. Finally, she asked if we could come later, in the afternoon. When we drove up to the house, she was out in the garden waiting. The two women fell into each other's arms, and we were led into the parlor for the grand confrontation.

Uncle Ignace was aroused from his nap. He came down the hall beaming. He was slight, wiry, and energetic. He held out his arms to his niece. They embraced. Then began an animated conversation that lasted through the afternoon and evening, almost nonstop, and left me more frustrated than if I had been watching a French movie without subtitles.

I begged my wife to interpret for me, especially when there was laughter, but she kept forgetting. She seemed to have a hard time translating into English, and I realized she had begun to think in French.

This more than once brought us close to disaster that morning as Uncle Ignace sat in the backseat of our car, giving directions which my wife was supposed to repeat in English.

"*A droite!*" he would shout.

"*A droite!*" she would echo, forgetting to translate.

"*A gauche!*"

"*A gauche!*"

I knew that *droite* means right and *gauche* means left, but I can't think in French, and by the time I translated

36 *gauche* into left or *droite* into right, it was too late. My confusion was compounded by the fact that *droit*—sans *e*—means straight ahead. How was I to know whether it had an *e* on it or not?

Once, as we approached a busy intersection, my wife shouted, *"C'est rouge! C'est rouge!"*

The red light was barely visible, and by the time I remembered that *rouge* meant red, I had already run it, leaving an outraged Frenchman beeping his horn behind me.

The road into the Pyrenees from Pau is very pretty, passing through several pleasant towns and villages. The scenery grew more mountainous and greener as we climbed toward Lees-Athas. The Pyrenees rise suddenly, dark green and stony. There was still snow on the higher peaks, perhaps in Spain.

We had gone about sixty kilometers from Pau when we came to Athas. (Lees, it turned out, was just a hayfield beyond it.) Athas was off the road to the right on a small plateau that tilted into a sheer stone mountain, startlingly close. Population had fallen so drastically that the two villages had combined. There were perhaps a dozen stone houses with dark slate roofs gathered around an old stone church. Nothing had changed in this century.

We drove through it, nodding to an old man sitting beside the road watching the traffic, which consisted solely of our car. Like the other men we were to see in Lees-Athas, he wore a black beret. As we entered the town, he was the only person we saw except for a handsome woman leading a horse down the road. We turned around and drove back to ask the old man which was the house of Professor Patie.

Professor Patie was the father of the woman at the tourist bureau. He had been the village schoolteacher, and now, in his eighties, he was retired. He received us warmly in a room with a fireplace, a dog, and a grandfather clock that might have ticked off every second since his birth. He was hardly more than five feet tall.

He had made himself the village archivist and correspondent for the newspaper in Pau. Proudly he opened a fat scrapbook to a story he had written about Joseph Casenave, my wife's other living uncle. It told how, belatedly, in 1980, Joseph had received *la médaille militaire* for heroism as a soldier in 1917. There was a picture taken of him for the story when he was eighty-two. The face under the black beret was weathered and hard, half scowling, half smiling at the camera. The stub of a cigarette was stuck in the center of his mouth.

Alas, Professor Patie told us, Joseph Casenave was not in the village. He had gone to visit a daughter in Pau. But we would walk up the road to his house, which assuredly was the Casenave house in which Suzanne Casenave was born.

We were in for another setback.

"He Looks Exactly Like My Mother!"

Our pilgrimage seemed at an end. We stood in front of an old stone house that Professor Patie identified as the birthplace.

The professor and I stood back, leaving my wife to her own emotions.

An old man walked toward us down the road—a dapper fellow wearing a jacket, pink sweater, gold-rimmed eyeglasses, and black beret. He was even older, I guessed, than the professor. He said good day and talked with the professor, evidently inquiring about the strangers. The professor explained. The older man shook his head and remonstrated with the professor.

Professor Patie talked to my wife. He seemed embarrassed. Her face fell.

She turned to me. "He says this isn't the house, after all."

When Joseph Casenave married, the old man had told

38 the professor, he moved into the house of his wife, which was only sensible, *n'est-ce pas?* This was the house of his wife. The house of the Casenaves was where it had always been—down the road and closer to the church. A short walk.

Our disheartenment was brief. We walked down the road, the old man leading the way. The two old villages known as Lees-Athas (population 200) lie up against the outer ramparts of the Pyrenees, their green fields walled in by the towering granite peak whose sheer face that morning was silver in the alpine air. The mountain seemed close enough to hit with a well-thrown stone.

The houses of Lees-Athas are gathered closely about its church. Many are two-story houses with the main rooms upstairs and large double doors downstairs to allow the sheltering of ploughs and animals. A few now shelter motorcycles or little cars.

It was to such a house that the old man led us. Indeed, he remembered Suzanne Casenave, and this was where she and all her brothers and sisters had been born and raised.

There were windows upstairs and the large double door below. The slate roof looked as silver as the mountain. Half the front was not plastered, and the rough stone masonry was exposed, giving the house a look of serene antiquity.

In its rude simplicity, so at home in its setting, the house was more pleasing to look at, I thought, more human in scale, and thus more poignant, than the extravagant chateaus we had seen.

My wife completed her meditation, perhaps trying to picture her mother leaving this house with all she possessed in a cardboard suitcase. Perhaps she had stepped into the church, which was only a door away, to pray for good fortune in America, and for those she might never see again.

We entered the church. It was the church in which Suzanne Casenave would have been baptized and had her First Communion. Its Gothic and Renaissance interior had recently been painted pastel colors. ("Everyone had to agree," Professor Patie said, "and to pay.")

In its size and simplicity, the church was more comprehensible to me than the cathedrals we had seen; if not as awesome, it was no less beautiful. Perhaps the sunny colors had chased away the incubus of ancient sins.

The birthplace had been found and contemplated. We had yet to meet a Casenave in the village. Uncle Joseph was visiting the daughter in Pau, and we were not to see him. But there was Louis, the son of Uncle Pierre.

Professor Patie led us to the house of Louis Casenave.

"My God," my wife said when he came to the door, "he looks exactly like my mother!"

"Une Autre Denise!"

Louis took us inside his house, and his wife set out their wines; then Louis put on his black beret and led us down the road to a field in which a woman was stacking mown alfalfa with a pitchfork. She was the woman I had seen leading a horse down the road and whose beauty I had noted. She was a strong-looking woman, but slender and supple; the village Ceres, goddess of the crops.

We headed toward her across the rough field. She stopped her work and watched us curiously. I stood back. Cousin Louis introduced my wife. The woman drove her pitchfork into the ground, flung out her arms, and shrieked, *"Une autre Denise!"*

The women embraced, laughing and talking joyously, two cousins named Denise, two women whose origins were the same but whose lives had been so different, separated by an ocean and a continent and by more than miles.

I was enchanted that Cousin Denise had the style to work in a hayfield in a print shift with little pink, blue, and yellow flowers. It had a slit up one side, and through it I saw a flash of white lace lingerie.

These two cousins named Denise were not so different. She pointed across the field to where a woman with a

40   pitchfork was pitching hay up to a man on top of a wagon. Two more Casenaves: another cousin, Jean, and his sister, Marie, who had never married.

We trooped across the field, and yet another dramatic scene was played out in that unlikely pastoral theater.

Finally, my wife said we must go. The hay must be got in.

Cousin Denise looked disappointed; she spoke. My wife answered.

"What did she say?" I asked a moment later.

"She said, 'You come and go like the whirlwind.'"

"What did you say?"

"I said, 'I'm coming back.'"

GETTING AROUND

You Have Suddenly Become a Complete Idiot

I had been home from the hospital only three weeks when my wife went to France. I knew I would miss her, but I insisted that she go. I threatened to die if she didn't, and in my condition, I was capable of it.

Our friends the Dalton-Coonradts picked her up to drive her to the airport, and I don't remember a more painful parting since the morning I caught a cab for the ship that was to take me to the Pacific in World War II and left her, pregnant, on a Powell Street curb in San Francisco.

I knew that if she gave up her odyssey to spend three weeks nursing a man who was feeble, depressed, self-pitying, boorish, demanding, and repulsive she might lose her own buoyancy. One of us had to stay afloat.

Her departure meant, though, that I would have to hire a nurse and a cook, and a driver to take me to my various doctors. I found all three in one—my cousin Annabel.

Annabel was born and raised in Shafter, a cotton and potato center northwest of Bakersfield. We were children together in the 1920s; she was always a favorite of mine.

For thirty-five years her mother was Shafter's librarian, and sometimes Annabel and I kept the library on Saturday afternoons when her mother went home to water the garden. Annabel was a tall, thin, freckled, red-haired girl, and I

42   can still vividly remember her marching along in her grammar school band. She played the slide trombone. It is a picture that illustrates for me the kind of quietly independent and spunky person she is.

Annabel is good-humored, tidy, soft-spoken, and unflappable. She enjoys small pleasures immensely and has a pervasive but gentle humor. She is widowed and retired and lives in a small apartment in Long Beach, a short boat ride away from a daughter and son-in-law in Avalon on Catalina Island.

Excepting my wife, she is surely the only person in the world who knows me well enough and has the temperament and stability to be virtually locked up with me for three weeks.

She drove up in her little white car the day after I came home, so my wife could go back to work, and stayed with me—cooking, dispensing my pills, shopping, feeding the dog, the birds, and the wild cats, watching television with me, answering the phone, and driving me about.

And listening to me.

I soon realized that my family was not as worried about me as much as they were about her. One of my sons called and asked me, "How's Annabel?" He sounded concerned.

I knew what he meant. He was wondering how Annabel was holding up under the strain. Evidently my very presence in a house can create an aura of tension. They didn't tell me at first, but gradually it has been coming out that I was an absolute monster in the intensive care unit at the hospital, wildly abusing everyone.

My French daughter-in-law, Jacqueline, told me later that when she came to see me in the ICU she said she was going to make me some tapioca pudding, and I loosed a tirade of vituperation against that humble dish and anyone who would concoct it.

"I wasn't myself," I told her.

In truth, though, I don't much care for tapioca pudding.

Actually, I believe I behaved toward Annabel with tact,

courtesy, and thoughtfulness. I tried not to complain. Even when I said I wanted apricots cut up in my mush, for the potassium, and she used fresh apricots instead of dried apricots. I never said a word except to insist that next time she use dried apricots.

For her part, she was exquisitely discreet. When I felt intellectually up to it, I left the Sunday crossword puzzle on the breakfast table and worked on it at breakfast and lunch. Between meals she would sometimes look at the puzzle and write out some of the answers on a sheet of paper. Then, when we sat down to eat, she would put the paper with her answers on the table near the puzzle, saying that she didn't know whether they were right or not, of course, and maybe I wouldn't even want to look at them. (They were usually right.)

The point is, she did not presume to fill in the answers on the puzzle itself, right or wrong. Had she done that, of course, our idyll would have been over, and I'd have had to send her home.

By the way, I was somewhat solaced for my poor performance on the crossword puzzle by a letter from J. W. McKelligott, a clinical psychologist. "What happens," he explained, "is that our capacity to cope with stress has diminished to the point where it is nearly non-existent. Even trivial matters appear to be enormously complicated and demanding. This problem is compounded by the fact that it is very difficult to explain to others why you have suddenly become a complete idiot."

I was also gratified by a letter from Virginia I. Strong, RN, of Tarzana, which helped to explain my behavior in the hospital. She wrote:

> I must be frank with you. I am a member of the international kidnaping ring that held you captive. . . . Nursing, particularly post-coronary bypass nursing, treads a fine line between care and coercion. I am not one of the nurses who actually gave you

44   direct care, but a sister to the philistine host at Huntington Hospital.

I, and most critical care nurses I know, often wonder what terrors are seen in the glazed, suspicious caverns of our patients' eyes when they awaken bound, gagged and pierced with pain, sound and sleeplessness. Too many victims are just inarticulate and some never survive the ordeal to recall the horrors of their timeless sojourn in darkness. Aside from my wild joy at your return, I am morbidly fascinated by your experience, which I so often orchestrate but never hear. Thank you for returning to my world. Thank you for remembering. Laugh often (it hurts but cures.)

One man wrote that he went crazy in the ICU and bit one of his nurses, among other outrages.

I wanted to bite one of my nurses, but she was always too quick for me.

One important emotional bond between Annabel and me was our common interest in the Lakers and the Dodgers. Alas, both of them were having a bad year. In the Laker-Celtic series we suffered through three of the most disappointing basketball games ever played and then caught the Dodgers in a fatal losing streak.

I was hoping to learn how to use my new state-of-the-art tape recorder during my convalescence, but it was still too complicated for me. I tried to show Annabel a tape I had made of *Three Days of the Condor,* but somehow I had got it interspliced with *North by Northwest,* and just when Robert Redford and Faye Dunaway were starting to make love, it switched to Cary Grant and Eva Marie Saint climbing down George Washington's nose on Mt. Rushmore.

My Favorite Places in L.A.

If you wanted to show a visitor Los Angeles, people often ask me, where would you take him? The *San Francisco Chronicle*'s resident poet, Herb Caen, before one of his rare and painful sorties into our wasteland, wrote ahead, asking if I had time to show him "my" Los Angeles.

Naturally, I tell visitors they might as well go to Disneyland and the Movieland Wax Museum and Mann's Chinese Theater, because that's where they really want to go and will go, anyway. Naturally, Herb Caen went where he wanted to go—to Ma Maison and Spago and other chic restaurants the insides of which I rarely see.

When my cousin Annabel was cooking and driving for me, in my wife's absence, I tried to take her to a few places to break the monotony of servitude for her. She lived in Long Beach, and except for the Music Center, Los Angeles was as alien to her as it was to Herb Caen.

I did not have the strength to set out on long adventures, so I tried to take her to places that were near my various doctors' offices so that when she drove me to my surgeon or my internist or my cardiologist or my nose man, there would be some small reward—for both of us.

My nose man was on Vermont, and before an afternoon appointment one day, I led her to Bullocks Wilshire, the most beautiful store I have ever seen; since San Francisco razed its City of Paris, it has no peer in the West. It is a precious museum piece of the 1920s art-moderne style, inside and out, and the miracle is that we have let it stand.

You no sooner enter than you are enveloped in perfumes from the cosmetics department, and your eye is dazzled by the zigzag interiors. It is like walking onto the set of a stylish apartment in an early 1930s movie.

We had lunch upstairs in the tearoom, nibbling at tiny shrimp and avocado and regarding the fashion show. *Très élégant.*

On another day after a morning appointment, we

46   lunched at a place whose name I can never remember, though I have sought it out several times when I happened to be in the neighborhood, usually for breakfast. It is not really a restaurant but a kind of fast-food stand that has the use of a pleasant courtyard inside a Spanish colonial-style storefront and office building on Wilshire across the street from the restored Wiltern Theater Building. There was a vogue for this hospitable style of architecture in the 1920s and 1930s, and dozens of examples of it remain on the western cityscape today.

You go into a small café off the courtyard and place your order at a counter, ordering from a menu on the wall, and pick up your sandwich or salad when your number is called and carry it out to the courtyard and sit in the open air under a palm tree near the fountain, listening to the water and the birds. Of course the *cuisine* isn't *nouvelle*.

I'm not urging anyone to go to this place. I'm only saying that the real charm of cities is not always in their famous places but in the hundreds of unheralded and unpretentious places that people discover and enjoy by themselves.

When I had to see my doctors in Pasadena, we had breakfast at the Konditori, on Lake Avenue, a Danish café that has tables and booths inside and a patio on the sidewalk with tables and umbrellas. You usually see people you know, because they keep coming back.

One Saturday morning after breakfast, I asked Annabel if she'd ever seen Caltech, it being nearby. No, she hadn't. How would a woman from Long Beach happen to see Caltech? And why?

We drove over and walked the length of the campus past the Millikan Library and along Olive Walk past the original gray Moorish-style buildings to the Athenaeum.

It might have missed some other parts of the metropolis, but spring had come in full flood to Caltech. The lawns were lush. The jacaranda trees were purple. The lilies in the ornamental pools were profuse and blooming in a palette of rich colors that even Monet could not have exaggerated.

We feasted our eyes on the Athenaeum standing at the ending of the lovely lane of olive trees. There is no more pleasing structure in the city than this old classic.

How wonderful, I thought, and promising for our society that this beauty had been created as a setting for the education of our very brightest young. But they probably wouldn't appreciate it until they were old grads and came back some Saturday morning in spring, like that day, and looked again.

One Monday, when I wanted to try an even longer walk, we went to the Arboretum. My cousin had never been there, either.

I led her over the walk and down the path to the Queen Anne cottage, which Lucky Baldwin had built in the eighties for his wife. We walked around the veranda and peeked into the windows at the mannequins in the furnished rooms and sat on a log looking out over the lagoon in the morning mist and listened to the ducks calling across the water and the screams of peacocks.

We were surrounded by 10 million people, and there was not another person in sight.

Another Glass of Chardonnay, S'il Vous Plait

I had hoped to slip back into society inconspicuously after my long withdrawal; but as it turned out, I had to wear a tuxedo my first time out.

My wife was somewhere in the Alps, 6,000 miles away, when we received an invitation to a black-tie reception at the Museum of Art for a preview of "A Day in the Country," the unprecedented exhibition of 127 French Impressionist paintings brought together from various collections around the world. Unfortunately, the reception was for the day after she was to arrive home, after three arduous weeks

LaLaLand

48 of hurtling about France in a rented Renault, and I expected that she would be in the throes of jet lag and exhaustion.

I told her about the invitation, though, when she phoned from Gap, her base of operations in the search for her father's native village.

"I'm afraid you'll be too tired to go," I said.

"I'll go if you have to drag me," she said, vastly overestimating my strength.

Actually, when we arrived at the museum and I saw that flight of stairs at the Ogden Drive entrance, I wondered if she wouldn't have to drag *me*. Halfway up, I realized that I had come out too soon. Few things remind a man of his limitations like a flight of stairs.

But of course it was worth the effort.

As art critic William Wilson wrote later in the *Times*, "Something infinitely reassuring sparkles from these paintings. . . ."

I may not know exactly what he meant by that, but I know what it means to me. Reassuring. That the earth is lovely. That life is a picnic. That the sun will shine.

Again, as Wilson said, "No wonder French Impressionism is everybody's favorite painting style. . . ."

It certainly is mine, which means, I suppose, that my taste is everyman's.

Sometimes I try to be different, though; which may be why I wore, instead of the obligatory black bow tie, a tie and cummerbund of rainbow colors. It seemed an appropriate occasion for going against tradition, as Édouard Manet had when he shocked the critics of Paris by painting his revolutionary picnic on the grass showing a nude young woman picnicking with fully dressed young men. The woman was not only out of her clothing but also out of proportion, which was regarded as worse.

The exhibition was wonderful: exciting and tranquilizing at the same time, like a picnic on the grass.

My wife, still disoriented from her long flight and suddenly surrounded by visions of Paris, the French countryside, and the seashore, must have felt even more strongly than I did the illusion of being there.

Of course it was too much for one evening. One might as well pass over France in a low-flying balloon. I thought the exhibition should stay in that one place forever so small children could grow up with it, as the children in Rome grow up kicking a soccer ball in the piazzas around Bernini fountains.

I saw one painting by Camille Pissarro that I knew and loved—a busy intersection in Paris from the perspective of an upstairs balcony or window. Where had I seen it? In a book? In the Louvre?

It turned out to be one of our own. Of course, I had seen it in this very museum, and I was quite sure I had seen it years before in the old museum at Exposition Park, before the great crosstown moving day.

Most of the paintings in the exhibition I would probably never see again, unless I could return that summer. Once the collection was broken up, it would be irreparably undone, like a broken egg, and would never be put together again.

It is said that there is some larceny in everyone's heart. I had to believe it when at last I stood before Claude Monet's *Terrasse à Sainte-Adresse.* It would be madness, of course, but I could imagine stealing it, just to look at it every day.

If there is any place in the world I might rather be than my own chair, it would be in the empty rattan chair on that terrace, beside the lady under the parasol, looking out across the water toward those pretty yachts and steamboats.

("Waiter, another glass of Chardonnay, *s'il vous plait,* and a Pernod for the lady.")

Of course if *Terrasse à Sainte-Adresse* were mine, I would give it to our own museum, scorning the millions it's probably worth; all I'd ask is that they rename the museum after me.

When we came out of the gallery onto the terrace, peo-

50 ple were still drinking and socializing. I supposed there was food, but I didn't see any empty tables, and I was getting cold. I dragged my wife down the stairs to the street.

We drove east on Wilshire, looking for a place to eat. Wilshire dies at night. Finally we found an open Bob's Big Boy. I had a tuna sandwich, and she had a spaghetti chili size.

I don't mean to knock Bob's; I often pick up lunch at a Big Boy. But somehow the meal didn't seem to fit the mood of the evening. Also, my wife had just come home from three weeks of French cooking.

A day or two later, I read in the *Times* that Rococo had catered the reception and that a "resplendent show of food" had been set out below the terrace in the atrium, complemented with Trefethen Eschol, an excellent California white.

I hoped my wife wouldn't read it, but of course she did.

Actually, my tuna sandwich wasn't all that bad.

"Piece of Cake"

After it leaked out that I was going to have a quadruple bypass and before I checked into the hospital, several old friends and a few strangers who had had heart surgery phoned to assure me that they never felt better in their lives.

One of them said he had just walked off the tennis court after three tough sets; another had just come out of the pool after doing twenty laps; didn't even sound winded. Two or three hinted that they were having terrific sex lives.

"Piece of cake," they said of the operation itself.

I was glad to hear from these fellows, and I looked forward to the buoyant recovery they all described. I thought I might be on the way when I did two laps in our thirty-five-foot pool, swimming slowly and close to the side. I used to do thirty laps—that is, ten laps three times a day. I would have been happy to do that again.

In that tense interlude before I went into the hospital, I especially relied on my old Belmont High School classmate Jerry Luboviski. Luboviski had been my first editor, on the Belmont *Sentinel,* and later, after World War II, I worked for him on two newspapers, including the old *Los Angeles Daily News.* He was one of the best newspapermen I ever knew, and I still listened to his counsel.

He came over to the house to talk to me before the operation. He had had a triple bypass twelve years earlier, when the operation was a novelty, and said he never felt better in his life than right now.

After I got home, I called him now and then for reassurance. Had he been terribly short of breath? Oh, yes. Couldn't walk across the living room without gasping. Had he been depressed? Oh, yes; terribly. But now here he was, walking four miles a day, taking trips around the world with Bonnie; I'd be okay.

When I needed him most, though, he failed me. I phoned one morning, worried about my inability to concentrate, and his wife said he was in the hospital. "He's got pneumonia," she said.

It wasn't anything mild. It was touch and go for a day or two. Then he pulled through, and a few days later he was home again. He phoned, sounding weaker than I did.

I wasn't finding the experience a piece of cake, but I thought that was more because of my psychological vulnerability than the physical trauma of the surgery. What ravaged me, as I've said, was my own delirium in intensive care and recovery and my frustration afterward, at home, when I was too weak and too distracted by the nose infection to do anything but watch TV, which very well might not only have retarded my recovery but also permanently damaged my brain.

What I am getting at now, though, is the curious occupations I found for that enfeebled brain. I couldn't just pace the floor, counting the minutes; I had to do something.

52   I thought of my pens and pencils. I had been working at the *Times* for thirty-one years, and it had been my habit to walk around with a pocketful of copy pencils and ballpoint pens, which the paper liberally supplies to editorial employees. I never meant to hoard these humble tools, but just accidentally bringing home one or two each week for what? —fifteen hundred weeks—I had collected more than I really needed. They were scattered around my workroom in large beer and coffee mugs—all mixed together.

One day, when I was still too fuzzy-minded to write a letter, I decided to sort them all out. I emptied the mugs on the dining-room table. There must have been two hundred pens and pencils. I know, it sounds like petty theft. But the collection had just grown.

I put all the empty cups in a row and set to work intently.

There were Eagle copy-desk pencils, yellow Dixon Ticonderoga pencils with erasers, and dozens of variously colored pencils that had found their way in from other sources; there were black pens, red pens, black and red felt-tipped pens, and dozens of retractable ballpoints, some of which I had bought, some of which were advertising giveaways.

I put all the yellow pencils in one mug, all the copy pencils in another, all the red pens in another, and so on, until I had a row of mugs, each filled with pens or pencils of the same type. There was of course a separate mug for commercial ballpoints and a separate cup for a few expensive prestige-name pens I had bought (though they were the valuable ones that usually got lost).

While I was at the height of this enterprise, which my cousin Annabel observed without comment, the phone rang. It was Luboviski.

We compared progress. He was better but still weak. He didn't feel like doing anything much.

"Me, too," I said. "You know what I'm doing?"

I told him. There was a long silence. I thought maybe he

had been distracted from the telephone. Then I could hear him laughing.

Finally, he said, "Can you believe this? I've been doing the same thing."

Luboviski had gone to work for the Union Oil Company about the same time I had gone to work for the *Times*, and evidently he had been just as sticky fingered with pens and pencils as I had.

It was a great morale booster to me. I felt that if my mind was coming along as fast as Luboviski's I would probably be all right.

And someday I'd look back on it all as a "piece of cake."

BRAIN DAMAGE

"You Mean Freddie?"

My doctors, perhaps for good reason, didn't warn me about one possible consequence of my bypass surgery—brain damage.

It is not, after all, an amusing subject, and I'd rather not mention it, but I'm afraid I might have suffered some and don't know it and some of my readers are beginning to wonder.

As I say, my doctors didn't say anything about it, and neither did any of the friends and well-wishers who wrote and telephoned me before the operation, telling me it was a piece of cake and that in two weeks I'd be playing tennis. (The only question was whether I'd be playing two sets or three.)

When I was home recuperating, though, I began receiving letters kindly advising me that I could expect some brain damage as a result of my heart's being stopped for several hours and my blood circulating through a machine.

One letter came from the office of a doctor in Newport who evidently specializes in writing and lecturing on this subject.

When enough people tell you that you've suffered brain damage, you begin to believe it. At least you begin to look

55

56   for symptoms and to see evidence of it in every mental lapse.

I have noticed that I have a hard time remembering names, even the names of people I know quite well, when I meet them suddenly under stress—if nothing more than the stress of a cocktail party.

I will suddenly look across the room at a man I have known for years and realize that his name has escaped me. I try the usual procedures recommended by the memory experts: Run through the alphabet and hope that a letter rings a bell. It doesn't. If the man's name is Fred Dalton, for instance, I will go right through F and D without a glimmer of recognition. Simply doesn't work.

Then panic rises in my breast like water in a flooding submarine, and I know my chances of remembering the fellow's name grow thinner as it rises. He is moving my way; a confrontation is unavoidable.

My only recourse is to avoid using his name altogether, but then some pushy person (whose name I can't remember, either) will move in and say, "How about introducing me to your friend, Jack?"

The only thing to do at this point is to move quickly away to the side of your wife and say, "Don't look now, but what's the name of that guy headed this way with the martini?"

"You mean Freddie?"

"Oh, yeah, Freddie. . . ." (Dalton-Coonradt, of course; you've only known him thirty-five years.) "Just slipped my mind."

A fine line of perspiration breaks out at the top of my forehead. What is the matter with me?

"I'm getting terrible at names," I confess.

My wife shrugs. "You always were."

If I have suffered brain damage, she says, it doesn't matter. I still have enough gray matter left for the things I use my brain for. I guess she means that if I were in some other line of work it might be more noticeable.

There may be other symptoms, but they may just signify senility. I am always going into a room and not being able to remember why I went into it. Sometimes I just stand there, when I realize I don't know what I had in mind, and it comes to me. Sometimes it never does.

I did have this trouble before surgery, though, and I can document that, because I have written about it before. In fact, I have a letter from a correspondent of mine, Martha Purviance, which shows that she was aware of that problem. She encloses a lament from the Yale alumni magazine that poignantly describes the syndrome:

> One of the most disturbing aspects of this age is my growing inability to recall important information, like the Greek alphabet, the gross national product of Lebanon and where I left my glasses.
>
> This becomes pronounced especially when I go upstairs to get something. Halfway up, I realize that I have no inkling of what I was going upstairs to get. Should I go back downstairs and try to remember what it was I needed? Or, should I continue going up and look for something that needs bringing down? Unable to decide, I resort to sitting on the landing, only to discover after three minutes that I have completely forgotten whether I originally was upstairs coming down, or downstairs coming up.

It was written by a Yale man, class of 1912.

It is easy to blame this fellow's difficulties on senility, since he would be at least in his eighties. But those paragraphs are too terse and graphic for a senile mind to have wrought, and I am inclined to think that their author may have suffered some damage to an obscure part of the brain that controls memory but has no effect on his prose. I hope that's all that is wrong with me.

Our cases are not, however, identical. I never have known the Greek alphabet, so could hardly forget it, and our house has no upstairs, which considerably simplifies my problem.

58   But I do spend at least three-quarters of an hour a day
looking for my glasses. That's half an hour looking for my
glasses and a quarter of an hour wondering what it is I'm
looking for.

I'd Come Up with Flora Bon Ami

My memory in some areas remains unimpaired. I can still
remember a few lines of Shakespeare; I can still recite the
first four lines of the prologue to Chaucer's *Canterbury
Tales;* I can still recall most of my vocabulary.

I can summon up such words as *labyrinthine* and *recon-
dite* when I need them and also hard ones like *preantepenul-
timate* (fourth from last) and *nilometer* (an instrument for
measuring the height of water in the Nile, especially during
its flood), even though they rarely come up.

Occasionally, however, as I have said, I get up out of my
chair and go into another room, and when I get into the
other room, I forget what I went into it for.

This type of memory loss is, of course, very common,
especially among people who are no longer in the bloom of
youth. According to a recent article on memory in *Newsweek,* memory begins to decline in the thirties. It is not true,
though, that the loss is continuous and serious with age.

I am encouraged by a current theory that older people
have trouble with short-term memory (STM) because they
have so much more to remember than the young. Consequently, they become selective and don't remember what
seems unimportant.

"Now," according to the article, "researchers are ques-
tioning whether memory deficits suggest that older adults
are smarter at figuring out what can safely be forgotten."

Only 1 percent of adults have a photographic memory,

Newsweek says. "The other 99% are plagued with forgetting."

Some people have a specific problem called prosopagnosia—they cannot recognize faces.

I must confess that I have this disease, though I had never heard the word before. I find it hard to remember people's names and to put names with the proper faces.

I meet many people at social events, many of them very charming and memorable; yet when I encounter these same people only a few weeks later, I cannot remember them.

Women come up to me smiling, with outstretched hands, and when I draw a blank, they will remind me that we sat next to each other at a luncheon a month before and had a wonderful conversation. It is very embarrassing.

Name cards are helpful, but when you have to bend over a woman and scrutinize her breast to read her name on a name card, you have lost whatever advantage learning her name might provide.

The important factor, according to *Newsweek*, is concentration. You must concentrate on the name when you are first introduced to someone, then try to associate it with something else.

Say you are introduced to someone named Poppy Bellamy. You think, "flower and *belle amie*," which I believe means "beautiful friend" in French. Then, when you meet her again, you remember flower and *belle ami*, and *voilà!* you have it.

It doesn't work. In that situation I would come up with Flora Bon Ami, or something equally disastrous.

Years ago I had a dentist who told me that another of his patients was a colleague of mine at the *Times*. "Bill Mudge," he said. "You know him?"

I knew him well. His name was Bill Dredge. I had no doubt that the dentist had used the association method to remember the name. "Dredge. What does a dredge do? It dredges up mud." So what he came up with was Mudge.

Many politicians have been successful mainly because of their ability to remember names. At social functions they

60   seem to remember the name of every important person. But I happen to know that many of these remarkable figures employ aides who stand at their elbows and whisper the names of anyone who approaches with hand extended. There are some otherwise inconsequential people who can develop that special skill. They become kingmakers.

My wife has always been good at names, and I count on her to perform this function for me. But we tend to get separated at parties, and I find myself suddenly in a wilderness of strangers.

I suggest, for the sake of all prosopagnosiacs, that everyone speak his own name when meeting anyone of only slight acquaintance.

All you have to do is smile and hold out your hand and say, "Hi. I'm Flora Bon Ami. We met at the Daltons."

Then I say, "Of course," as if I had never doubted it. "I'm Jack Smith."

And then I wander off, wondering what I'm doing there in the first place.

I Still Know Who the Person in My Wife's Bed Is

Evidently the loss of short-term memory is as common as a headache or a cold.

Many readers have added their complaints to mine about forgetting what one has gone into another room for and not being able to remember names and faces.

Several have little routines for remembering what they have gone into another room for.

Helen Colton of Family Forum (nonprofit adult education) says one of her students suggested that when you get up to go into the other room you should say out loud, over and over, what it is you're going for.

"So, many times a day, I walk through my house talking

out loud to myself. 'A cup of coffee.' 'A toothpick in the kitchen drawer.' 'Turn on the laundry machine.' You know what, Jack? It works."

Another simple routine works for Roberta Diamond. "Please don't laugh at this. It really works. When you forget what you went into another room for, don't fret. Just go back to the room you got the original thought in and, believe it or not, it will come back to you."

Caroline T. Bales of Alhambra also recommends retracing your steps: "All you have to do to remember is to go back to where you were (your chair) and you will immediately remember what you went to the kitchen to get or to do."

Okay. But what if you forget where you came from?

Visualization does it for Edward A. Westphal of San Clemente. He says a memory expert taught him that when he decides to go into another room for something—a book from the bookcase in the library, a tool from the workshop —first to visualize himself standing in front of the bookcase or tool rack and visualizing the object he has in mind. Takes only a couple of seconds, and it works, he says.

Like me, others have had trouble trying to remember names by word association. Evidently the ministry is a perilous profession in this regard, since ministers are expected to remember the names of their congregations.

Reeta Rundlett of Claremont tells of the parson who tried to remember the name of a new member, a Mrs. Lumach, by associating it with stomach. When he met her next, he said, "Good morning, Mrs. Kelly!"

Myra Huffman of Laguna Hills, whose mother was a minister's wife, recalls that her mother used word association on her husband's congregation. One Sunday she met a new member named Davenport, and the next Sunday greeted her with "Good morning, Mrs. Sofa!"

I would probably have called her "Mrs. Chesterfield."

Roger Arnebergh, former Los Angeles city attorney, recalls that he used to meet many people when he spoke in public. Later, when accompanied by his wife, he would meet

some of them again but would have forgotten their names. Common courtesy required that he introduce his wife.

"How did I handle the situation? I cordially said, 'Well, hello, you remember Emilie?' as I turned to her. Invariably he would say, 'Certainly,' and usually introduce himself to her."

That's okay if you're married.

Ed Shoaf recalls how one politician coped with this embarrassing situation. He would say to the *other* man, "Hello, how's Muriel?"

I can't see how that would solve the problem. But its merit may have been that it would create another problem altogether.

By eavesdropping, Joan La Cour discovered James Roosevelt's method for seeming to remember people who lined up to shake his hand. Roosevelt shook each person's hand, then said a few words that invariably caused the person to brighten.

"Edging closer, I heard Mr. Roosevelt say, as he shook the hand of the person next in line, 'How *are* you? Is that pesky cold gone?' "

And to the next person he said, "All over that head cold?"

Later, La Cour asked Roosevelt how he did it. "It's a pretty safe bet that every one of these people has had a cold some time in the past couple of years," he said. "I've never been wrong yet."

On such devices political careers are made.

One wonders at the ability of actors to remember their lines. I have a recurring nightmare of being in a college play and not knowing my lines.

Writes Charlton Heston:

Recalling and interpreting blocks of text is what I do for a living. I don't study lines, I don't forget lines, but that's all my memory does well.

I read somewhere that the brain is something like a muscle and thus does well what it has been trained to do. Memorizing text, in my case. For everything else, people have to pin notes to my lapel.

Heston recalls standing at a crosswalk on Sunset Boulevard with Walter Seltzer, a producer who knew his weakness. When the light changed, Seltzer gripped his arm and said, "Chuck! There's Howard Koch crossing towards us. You know him well. He's head of Paramount, where we're about to start filming."

" 'Oh, for Pete's sake!' I said. 'I know Howard!' I then embraced a complete stranger."

Sarah Conrad of Glendale reassures me that I don't have prosopagnosia, the disease that causes one to forget faces.

She says,

A person with prosopagnosia has difficulty recognizing family members, well-known persons, and in extreme cases, his own face. . . . So unless you wonder who that strange lady in your wife's bed is or you wondered who that person on TV giving the State of the Union address was, you don't have prosopagnosia.

My memory may not be perfect, but at least I still know who the person in my wife's bed is.

HOLLYWOOD THEN

"Hollywood, Not Hollyweird"

I drove out to Hollywood the other day to see if B. Dalton's had a copy of *The Last Tycoon*, F. Scott Fitzgerald's unfinished novel (they did), and stopped in to see the renovated Hollywood Roosevelt Hotel. Somebody must have had faith in Hollywood: the purchase and renovation of the hotel, according to a brochure I picked up, cost $35 million.

Anyone who thinks that Hollywood Boulevard is dead should pay the Roosevelt a visit. The elaborate coffered ceiling of the lobby has been thoroughly restored, and a three-tiered fountain splashes at the center under the original chandelier. It gleams with newness and inspires with spacious vaulted rooms, period grandeur, and a haunting memory of Hollywood past.

If Franklin Delano Roosevelt wasn't a favorite of yours, don't let that stop you. The hotel was built in 1926, in the golden era of Los Angeles architecture, and it was named after Teddy Roosevelt, not Franklin.

I walked into the dining room. It was bright and elegant, with pink napery on the tables. A young woman came toward me, smiling.

"I'm just looking," I told her. "At the renovation. It's beautiful."

65

66   "Yes," she said. "We want it to be Hollywood again—not Hollyweird."

I walked up tile-and-terra-cotta stairs to the mezzanine and looked down at the lobby glowing under the chandelier. Around the walls of the mezzanine they had hung a historical exhibition: the story of Hollywood in—what else?—pictures.

I walked slowly around it, stopping before the images that were still so touching:

The wonderful facade of the Egyptian Theater before its fragmentation. It had been built in 1922, the year King Tuthankhamen's tomb was discovered, at the height of the Egyptian craze that swept America.

The upstairs Montmartre, also built in 1922, where Valentino danced, Bing Crosby sang with the Rhythm Boys, Gloria Swanson lunched, and Joan Crawford often won the Charleston contests at the tea dansants.

The Trocadero, Ciro's, and the Mocambo, which was described as "a cross between Imperial Rome, Salvador Dali and a bird cage."

The Hollywood Canteen, converted from a barn at Sunset and Cahuenga. At its wartime peak, it was visited by 100,000 servicemen a month. Danny Kaye, Red Skelton, Kay Kyser, and Rudy Vallee entertained for free, and Rita Hayworth, Bette Davis, or Marlene Dietrich might be found washing dishes in the kitchen.

D. W. Griffith's massive outdoor set for *Intolerance.* He recreated Babylonia right here in Hollywood, complete with slaves and dancing girls.

The talkies. What a shock to the silent world of motion pictures! "Al Jolson sings!" "Harold Lloyd talks!" Many scoffed, but *Fortune* magazine declared: "Beyond comparison the fastest and most amazing revolution in the whole history of industrial revolution."

In the beginning Hollywood had been called "La Nopalera," meaning "cactus patch," after the Nopal cactus that grew abundantly on its hills. It was pioneered by a Kansas prohibitionist, Harvey Henderson Wilcox. He subdivided a tract in the Cahuenga Valley and sold the lots to midwestern friends who practiced his Methodist morality. His wife, Daeida, named it Hollywood.

Midwestern morals went down the drain in the early 1900s when five-cent movie theaters called nickelodeons became the rage. Dozens of these "theaters" appeared overnight in store fronts. Patrons paid a nickel to get in and sit on camp chairs to watch jerky briefs on a white sheet, with no ventilation.

The Garden of Allah, a group of cottages built around a bar and pool in 1921 by Alla Nazimova and frequented by such illustrious revelers as Orson Welles, F. Scott Fitzgerald, Ramón Navarro, Clara Bow, Leopold Stokowski, Gene Fowler, Robert Benchley, and Charles Butterworth. I'd rather have spent an hour at that bar than in the arms of Helen Twelvetrees. (But I'd hate to have had to make that choice.)

I wanted to take some notes but found that I didn't have a notebook. I didn't even have an envelope to write on. I walked into a small office where a woman was just starting to make a phone call. She put the phone down and looked up.

"I wonder if you'd be good enough to give me a scrap of paper," I said. "I'd like to take some notes on the exhibition."

She riffled through a drawer and pulled out an unused remnant of a stenographer's notebook.

"Is this all right?" she asked.

She was as pleasant as the hostess had been in the dining room. I got the impression that these people were really trying to make Hollywood hospitable.

On the sidewalk, as I left the hotel, I stepped on the star of Lily Pons. I walked to my car and drove a few blocks down the boulevard to Musso & Frank Grill which had also been in the exhibition. It was a survivor, too. It had been in the same location since 1919 and still had the same wooden booths. In the 1930s it had been much frequented by Fitz-

68 gerald, Faulkner, Benchley, and other famous writers who had been lured to Hollywood to write for the movies.

I parked in back and went in and sat at the counter and had the chicken salad. I looked around for Scott and Bob and any other of my heroes that might be there, but I didn't see anyone I knew.

There's a new crowd now.

Where to Sin

Writer Leslie Raddatz has been digging in neglected sections of his bookshelves and turned up a little book a friend had picked up years ago in a secondhand bookstore and passed on to him.

It is called *How to Sin in Hollywood* and was published in 1940, the year before Pearl Harbor.

Raddatz has sent me copies of several of the more nostalgic pages, each of which is a sketch of some night spot that is recommended for the native or the tourist who hankers for a taste of genuine Hollywood night life, with sin thrown in.

We all know that the dollar isn't what it used to be; but even with our memories of the rock-bottom days of the Great Depression it is almost funny to read the prices extant in 1940.

Almost incredibly, some of the night spots listed in the book are still in business, at the same locations, but of course the style of entertainment has changed, and the prices are of another order of magnitude altogether.

Some of them twanged the strings of my memory, especially the Seven Seas, which was at 6904 Hollywood Boulevard, across from Grauman's Chinese Theater.

"This is long, low, narrow, dark, intimate, hot, feverish, and . . . Hawaiian," says the author in his feverish style. "This is a secret place, much bambooed, where amateur beachcombers come to make passes at amateur mermaids. . . ."

I never made any passes at amateur mermaids in the Seven Seas, but I spent some hours sitting at the bar, brooding like any lonely beachcomber, and waiting for the tropical squall. There was a tin canopy over the bar, and every few minutes an artificial rainstorm would come, drumming on the canopy like the rain on the roof of the Pago Pago hotel in Somerset Maugham's "Miss Sadie Thompson."

It was a great hangout during the war for soldiers and sailors on leave from the Pacific or on the verge of going out there. I believe I last sought out the sanctuary of the Seven Seas in 1946, when I had left my pregnant wife and our first child in San Diego and come up to Los Angeles to seek my fortune.

It took me back to our two years in Hawaii, when we had lived for a time in a real grass shack on the lagoon at Sans Souci, toward Diamond Head from Waikiki. The rain on our roof had been one of the natural wonders of life in the islands.

According to *How to Sin in Hollywood*, drinks at the Seven Seas in 1940 were thirty-five cents and up.

Perino's, at 3927 Wilshire Boulevard, was in full flower in 1940. "Here comes the Great Garbo to dine in suave seclusion," the author writes with breathless reverence. "Here comes the Great Chaplin, chatting in a corner quietly with (his) radiant Goddard . . . Here come the Great Tycoon, his Great Dowager, their Great Deb—"

But it would cost you to dine in such company: Lunch was $1.25, dinner $2.00 and up. Drinks 35 cents and up. One was urged to "try the pheasant."

I actually took my bride to Perino's on our wedding trip, though it made a noticeable dent in the $100 I had set aside for that odyssey. I had always regarded the Ambassador Hotel as the height of luxury and elegance, but of course we couldn't afford to stay there. So we stayed a night at the William Penn, over on Eighth Street, and walked through the lobby of the Ambassador, as if we were guests, and dined at Perino's. I still remember the shock when I

70   discovered that a cup of coffee after dinner cost twenty-five cents.

By the way, we did not see Charlie Chaplin or Greta Garbo or even the radiant Goddard.

Chasen's, at 9039 Beverly Boulevard, where it still stands today, was already the cynosure of the stars. "Bette Davis, Marlene Dietrich, Darryl F. Zanuck, Peter Lorre, Thomas Mitchell, Mary Astor and friends are gossipping, arguing, holding hands, hailing from table to table. . . ."

It was expensive. Drinks, forty cents and up. Dinner à la carte. "Figure $3 for a good meal."

I had never been in Chasen's until several years ago, when I was introduced to its famous chili by Jet Fore, the last of the great Hollywood press agents.

I hope they haven't made the mistake, like Coca-Cola, of changing their chili.

Ciro's was at 8433 Sunset Boulevard, on the Strip. It was The Place where celebrities went to see and be seen. You had to be making it, or on a big expense account, to go there. It was *soigné*. Recommended dress for Saturday nights was "Tux or better."

Jim Moran, the great clown and impostor, was wearing "better" the night he dressed up as an Arabian prince and, pretending an accident, spilled a bag of sparkling jewels on the floor. The scramble that followed, with alleged celebrities on their tuxedoed knees, scooping up what turned out to be glass, proved Moran's moral, that Hollywood's classiest would grovel for riches.

Then there was Earl Carroll's, famous for its boast "Through these portals pass the most beautiful girls in the world." Alas, I never put it to the test, though there was a minimum charge of only one dollar, and drinks were thirty-five cents and up.

Several of the great spots of forty-eight years ago survived until very recently; Musso and Frank is still there, on the boulevard, since 1919; Don the Beachcomber is gone, along with the Cock 'n' Bull on Sunset, along with such habitués as Ronald Colman, Leslie Howard, Madeleine Carroll, David Niven, and C. Aubrey Smith; Lawry's Prime Rib, which used to offer ribs at $1.25, drinks 20 cents and up, is still in business on La Cienega.

Most lamented of those that have gone, I would say, would be Slapsie Maxie's. Slapsie Maxie's presence was the reason for its being. Joe E. Brown, Martha Raye, and the Ritz Brothers used to come to see Rosenbloom, the former light heavyweight champion of the world, do his "impoisonations" of Little Lord Fauntleroy, Al Jolson, the Great John L., and Maurice Chevalier.

I always ate at Thrifty's. Sin was beyond my means.

Garbo in Boxer Shorts

Celebrities today are not as real and accessible as those of times past.

Unlike the Greek gods, they do not come down to earth to mingle with ordinary people. They exist on a surreal plane and are seen only as images on screens or the pages of magazines.

Those who do come to earth do it only in enormous settings, like the Coliseum or Dodger Stadium, where they appear at a distance from the multitudes.

One hardly hopes to bump into Prince shopping at K Mart or to Madonna looking into Frederick's window on Hollywood Boulevard, or even on Rodeo Drive.

One way to remain a celebrity is to remain remote; to give the impression of otherworldliness, of being not quite real and mortal.

One of the fantasies of people who live a long way from Los Angeles is that we who live here are all acquainted with celebrities and rub elbows with them every day.

I remember capitalizing on this myth shamelessly when I was a very young man in the merchant marine. One night at a dance in Melbourne an Australian girl asked me if I

knew Robert Taylor. I told her that I not only knew him but lived next door to him.

She evidently believed me. Los Angeles was far away, a fairy-tale land where anything was possible.

Mary R. McCormick writes that she *did* see Garbo at Perino's. She and a sorority sister from Kansas were splurging for lunch at that soigné restaurant, and the maître d' discreetly informed them that Garbo was lunching with a gentleman friend a few tables away.

Observing the great star surreptitiously, the two young women noticed that she tasted every dish on her companion's plates. "She was indeed gorgeous and wore no makeup whatsoever . . ."

Ann Bricka of Long Beach remembers an even more intimate glimpse of Garbo.

> Many pounds ago (1938–41) I was a model for Saks in Beverly Hills. Every day at noon we would show the latest fashions in Perino's tiny satellite restaurant on the top floor. Many stars dropped in to lunch in its quiet seclusion.
>
> One day Garbo was there and liked the white crepe shirtwaist evening gown I was modeling. She said she would like to try it on, so I took her to my dressing room, where she disrobed to only a pair of men's white boxer shorts. They were very fine, not your Fruit of the Loom at all. There was no bra (a bit of trivia you might find interesting).

Which brings us to Ray Bradbury. "Nostalgia freaks," he writes, "step aside. I can top you all."

> One twilight, back in late 1938, if I recall correctly, I came out of the big downtown library (my university) and walked down past the Biltmore Theater. Katherine Cornell was there in, I believe, "Candida." The matinee was just breaking, and in the dusk, as I approached the front entrance of the

theater, I could hear the doors opening and the crowd beginning to exit. As I reached the blind corner of the entrance, I heard running feet and a woman in a large hat, her head down as if plowing the wind, ran right into my suddenly opened arms. The woman, surprised at my catching her, raised her head and I looked into the face and the great eyes of:

Greta Garbo.

It was only a moment, perhaps two seconds, three.

Then she burst off and ran across the street into the Biltmore garage.

I found out later that Garbo often attended theater matinees and sat in the last row so she could run out ahead of the mobs.

I never saw Garbo again.

But I shall remember our swift embrace for the rest of my life.

I have had several encounters with stars of the first order—besides those brought about by my access as a reporter.

Not long ago I was shopping for a printer in a computer store and ran into Marlon Brando. He was wearing a planter's hat, which fit his image as a South Seas island owner, and he was deeply engrossed with a salesman on the merits of various pieces of equipment.

That's what people all over the world think we do. We run into Marlon Brando in a store.

Once, more than thirty years ago, I was sitting alone in a bar in Studio City, in the afternoon, having a beer, when a man came in and sat two stools away from me. He ordered a beer, and we looked at each other in the backbar mirror.

It was Robert Mitchum.

He knew I knew who he was, and I knew he knew. I assumed that if he wanted to say hello he would. He didn't, and I didn't.

74   My one encounter with Jean Simmons had an even bleaker ending. I was pursuing some visiting royalty through Twentieth Century-Fox studios, where Simmons was making *Desirée* (with Brando as Napoleon). She came up behind me, tapped me on the shoulder, and when I turned around, she held a cigarette to her lips and said, "Do you have a light."

I didn't.

DISASTER

In a Sense, I Was Dead

After recovering from my bypass surgery, I confronted my surgeon and asked him why that ordeal had been necessary.

"When you told me I needed the operation," I said, "I didn't argue. I didn't demand a second opinion. I didn't read the literature. I didn't consult my friends. I just said 'When do you want to do it?' and you said, 'Tuesday.'

"Now I want to know why we did it."

The surgeon said, "I can promise you one thing. You won't die of a heart attack."

Good news, I thought, though it occurred to me vaguely that I would have to find something else to die of.

My heart attack came on a Sunday in December. I was at home watching a Ram football game on television. I was in the bedroom, on my electric bed, reading the paper and drinking black coffee and watching the game—my usual routine on a Sunday morning in football season.

My wife was in her bathroom feeding her parakeets and the cockatiel.

Suddenly I started coughing and felt short of breath. With each breath it grew shorter. I cried out to my wife. I told her to call the doctor.

She led me to the kitchen to be by her side while she called on the wall phone. She got his answering service.

75

They were trying to reach him. I was growing worse. It felt as if something were rising in my lungs, making my breathing ever more shallow, until I was just taking in air in short gulps.

"You hold this," she said, handing me the phone, "in case he comes on. I'm going to call the paramedics."

She went into my den to use our other line.

She got back and took the phone from me before the doctor came on. Then she was talking to him, telling him she had already called the paramedics. "Yes, yes," she said. "All right."

She said he'd be waiting for us at Huntington Memorial Hospital.

I was gasping for every breath. She led me to the couch by the front door and opened the door, and we waited.

I grew weaker by the moment. I couldn't think. I toppled over.

She grabbed me and held me up and said, "Hold on, Jack, oh, hold on!"

She kept holding me, saying "Why don't they come!" Finally, she cried, "Hold on, Jack! Oh, God, hold on! I can hear the siren—they're coming!"

From there things merge into blackness for me. I faintly remember being taken up in a man's arms. They said later, on their chart, that I was talking. But I don't remember anything. Not even the ambulance ride. Not even the siren.

I don't remember anything of the next two days.

Piecing it together from the charts and from my family's recollections and some of the doctors' and nurses', this is what happened.

First to arrive at our house was a fire truck. My wife can't remember what they did to me, but they had come, evidently, because there are more fire stations than paramedic stations and they have a better chance of getting there first. In a minute or so the paramedics arrived.

My wife told them they were waiting for me at Huntington, but they said they had to take me to the County-USC Medical Center, because it was closer. They couldn't take her in the ambulance, but the fire truck led her over in her car. (Every time we pass a fire truck today she blows the crew a kiss.)

On the way to the hospital the paramedics made contact with a nurse who took my symptoms and ordered treatment. When I reached emergency, I was described as being in severe respiratory distress. My heart was fibrillating, and I went into congestive heart failure. My heart stopped.

Clinically I was still alive; but in a practical sense, I was dead.

The doctor on duty ordered electric shock treatment to restore my heartbeat. A nurse placed two metal plates on my chest and gave me a jolt. Nothing happened.

"Again," the doctor told her. She gave me another jolt. My heart began to beat again in a regular rhythm.

Finally, I was moved up to the intensive care unit, where my wife was first able to see me. I wasn't much to see. I was described on the charts as cold and blue, with no response to stimuli and no palpable pulses; my extremities were extended and my fists clenched. My eyes were closed.

Somewhere along here, with my wife's signed permission, they inserted an arterial pump in my leg to assist my heart in pumping blood. It was coordinated with my heartbeat and was attached to a monitor that had to be watched constantly.

For six hours I was comatose. For all I knew, I was dead. One foot was on the other shore, and the man in the dark suit had hold of one of my hands.

I remember absolutely nothing of this period. No soft lights. No golden horizons. No heavenly Muzak. No angels singing. I don't remember it, but when I opened my eyes at last, my wife was standing at my bedside holding one of my clenched hands, and my son Curt was holding the other. They said I opened my eyes and squeezed their hands, and they knew I had come back.

My recovery was remarkable. I remained in intensive care, with my artificial heart pumping in my leg and a dozen tubes delivering and relieving me of various fluids and de-

78   prived of my favorite weapon—my power of speech. A tube ran down past my voice box and into my lungs to keep me in oxygen.

A nurse noted on her chart: "Patient awake, alert & oriented. Responds appropriately to verbal questions. Communicates with writing pad. Nods head and attempts to talk frequently."

On the following Friday they decided I was stable enough to move out of intensive care. The tube had been removed from my mouth, which let me talk, and according to my daughters-in-law, made me sound like my old, impatient, irascible self.

They moved me to Huntington Memorial by ambulance, but I don't even remember the ride.

Alive in La La Land

I spent Christmas week in the intermediate-care unit at Huntington. They had put me back in my old room overlooking a part of the rooftop, with a piece of snow-capped mountain in the distance.

I had a couple of tubes spliced into my veins, and I was wired to a monitor in the nursing station, and every half hour or so they came for my vitals and a sample of my blood; but altogether it wasn't unpleasant.

I was alive, a fact that I began to savor as a Christmas present. I had arrived at the medical center as good as dead, and they had saved my life. To them, it was routine.

They hadn't taken any time, I imagined, to consider whether my life was worth saving. It was just what they did, all day long, day after day. What I did with my life, once they had given it back to me, was up to me.

I felt that I had been for a moment on the outward shore. I had heard of many people who had come back with fanciful tales of what they saw; but I had beheld no wonders. Nothing. Just the void. Oblivion.

I couldn't remember what my last words had been before the paramedics picked me up at our house on Mt. Washington. They say I was babbling. I was not thinking about living, not thinking about dying; just fighting for breath. My mind was fading.

I didn't even think to say, "I'm dying," much less to say something decent to my wife like "I love you" or even "Thanks."

I have always been skeptical of those famous last words attributed to famous men in their death throes. More likely, I suspect, at the last they were like me—simply suffocating and losing their mental grasp while they fought for breath.

My wife had virtually moved into the medical center while I was there. Now she came to see me every day, though I tried to get her to go home or go to work and get me off her mind. Obviously, I was going to live and be as mean as ever.

One afternoon my bypass surgeon came to see me. He seemed to be annoyed about something.

"You didn't have a heart attack," he said. Evidently he remembered promising me that I wouldn't die of a heart attack and had read that little notice in the *Times* that said I had suffered a heart attack and was in serious condition.

"I didn't?" I said, really quite surprised.

"No," he said. "That wasn't a heart attack."

"What was it, then?" I asked.

"That was an arrhythmic episode." he informed me.

Suddenly I knew what I would finally die of: semantics.

Christmas Eve my wife brought me a green blazer I had admired at Gary Lund's and also a bottle of Chardonnay to share with me over my hospital dinner. Before she showed me the wine, she had asked my cardiologist about it, following him out into the hall, and he had said, "Why not?"

Actually, it wasn't very good Chardonnay, which she realized at the first sip.

"I told him I wanted good Chardonnay," she said. "He said, 'How much did you want to spend?' and I said, 'Oh, seven or eight dollars.' "

So that was it. She knew the taste of a good Chardonnay, but she was out of touch with the price of a good Chardonnay. That was what had come of my doing the shopping for all our wine and spirits. So much for my honorable attempt at sharing the household responsibilities.

Even though it wasn't vintage, I drank one glass of it, she drank the rest, and we had a merry Christmas.

In the flush of celebration she talked more freely than before about our recent experience. It hadn't been easy for her. When I lay in a coma, the doctor had told her my condition was "grave" and hinted that if I did live I might suffer brain damage.

As she stood by the bed, holding my stiffened hand, she didn't know what to expect if I woke up.

I hadn't known, or didn't remember having been told, that my heart had fibrillated and stopped. I hadn't known about the shock treatment to get it started. I knew only that I had had something called pulmonary edema and congestive heart failure. I knew also that I had been through the void and in that first week I had felt life returning to me, weak and giddy as I was.

When she left that Christmas Eve to go home, I was suddenly very lonely and anxious. What had caused my heart to flip out of rhythm like that? What if I really had suffered brain damage? How would I know? They had taken a scan in the Huntington and found that I hadn't suffered a massive myocardial infarction, which would have resulted in severe heart damage. So I might be almost as good as before. But whatever happened could happen again, couldn't it?—maybe right now.

That night I called for my sleeping pill.

On Saturday before New Year's week I was stable enough to be sent home. The house seemed wonderful. A wonderful place to live. My den was just as I had left it. In idiosyncratic disorder.

Immediately I began to see things that needed doing. Let's get rid of that big stereo—TV console, I told my wife; put in a smaller TV and some more record cases. I'm going to get a big brown leather recliner for my reading corner. And let's get rid of that orange couch; get something bigger and maybe not so bold. She got into the spirit of it. She'd been thinking of getting rid of the old draperies she'd made and replacing them with slatted blinds.

I realized what I was doing. I had been given a new run on life. I wanted to use it. To change things. To create. If only by changing the furniture around.

On Monday my wife said, "You didn't shave today?"

"Can't you tell?" I said. "I'm growing a beard."

It was something else I could do. I could grow a beard. I was the master of my soul. It was the best of all possible worlds.

I was alive in La La Land.

"We Can't Slow Down, Herb"

On New Year's Eve I had a hard time controlling my emotions. I was overcome by the wonder of being alive, of having made it through the year.

And I felt confident that I was going to make it through another. The worst year of my life was over, and I had survived it. Surely the man in the dark suit was discouraged; he had let me slip away on our last appointment, and he knew I wasn't likely to get that close again for a while.

While my wife was preparing dinner, I got out some Beethoven albums, thinking it would be good to finish off the old year in a burst of fine music, then enter the new one on the great turbulent wave of the Ninth Symphony, rolling in on that magnificent supercharged chorus singing the "Ode to Joy."

I played the Seventh first. It is so splendid; it would show that I still had some respect for the old year. But it was too much for me. My emotions were too close to the surface. That rhythmic buildup toward melodic splendors to come was more than I could handle. I was overcome,

near tears; and when the phone rang, I turned the music off so I could talk.

It was Herb Caen, calling from San Francisco. We are supposed to be adversaries, he being the voice of San Francisco, Baghdad by the Bay, the Paris of the West, and I the defender of Los Angeles, the great wasteland. Of course it is nonsense. I admire Caen as one of the nation's most popular and skillful columnists; and personally, I love him.

He wanted to know how I was and to wish me a happy New Year. I told him I was all right and was going to go back to work soon.

"Don't you think you ought to slow down?" he said.

"Herb," I said, knowing he had been around as long as I had, "have you ever slowed down?"

"Well, no," he said. "I guess not."

"We can't slow down, Herb."

"I know it," he said.

I put the Beethoven albums away and got out an album of Irving Berlin, one of Cole Porter, and the sound track of *Pennies from Heaven*, with all that wonderful old stuff in it.

That was more like it. Beethoven was the music of the spheres. Irving Berlin and Porter were the music of my life, of the streets and alleys and bars and proms and rumble seats and barracks and living rooms I knew.

"Cheek to Cheek" . . . "I've Got My Love to Keep Me Warm" . . . "All Alone" . . . "What'll I Do?" . . . "Did You Ever See a Dream Walking?" . . . "Let's Fly Away" . . . "Just One of Those Things."

I decided to open a bottle of champagne. We were going to celebrate alone. We had had to turn down our usual New Year's Eve parties, and our sons and daughters-in-law were going to be with friends of their own generation.

I went into the kitchen and asked my wife: "If I opened a bottle of champagne, could you drink three-quarters of it?"

She said: "I could sure try."

That's one of the many things I had always liked about

her. She had always been willing to do more than her share, and cheerfully.

I got out a bottle of the champagne I usually have in stock for festive occasions and started to open it. But I had been warned against doing anything strenuous, and I noticed I was straining, trying to get the cork out.

"I'm afraid I can't do it," I said to her. "You think you could?"

"I'll try," she said. "I really don't know how. I've never opened champagne. I've always been afraid of it."

I felt a little surge of pride. You couldn't say a man was a complete failure as a husband if in forty-five years of marriage his wife hadn't once had to open a bottle of champagne.

She struggled with it, but finally there was a gratifying pop; she didn't even get an overflow.

I got out two champagne flutes and filled one for her and poured just enough in the other to make a toast.

We raised our glasses, and I said, "Happy New Year." I don't believe in elaborating on the traditional language of such occasions. We drank.

On the phonograph Rudy Vallee was singing "Let's Put Out the Lights and Go to Sleep" in that reedy but strangely vital and exhilarating voice of his.

As it turned out, my wife drank seven-eighths of the champagne, and after dinner she got to talking about our recent experience. She had been so emotionally strung out that she couldn't remember much more about the first day than I could.

But she remembered coming home from the hospital Monday morning to get some fresh clothes and seeing an envelope that I had left Sunday morning, before I was stricken, for the postman to pick up on Monday.

It was a renewal of my subscription to the *Skeptical Inquirer.*

At first she was going to take it back. That was her French frugality. Why waste it if I might not be coming home? Then she realized that that was a betrayal. She let it

84   go. I was entitled, even at the end, to renew my faith in skepticism.

We put out the lights and went to sleep before the year ended.

At midnight we were awakened by the whistling and merrymaking in the neighborhood.

"Is that it?" she said.

"That's it," I said, feeling safe.

I had escaped the year alive.

SAMANTHA

"Miracle Is the Name of the Dog"

One weekend our French daughter-in-law, Jacqueline, drove down to our house in Baja with five women friends, and naturally I was anxious until I heard from her the morning after they came back.

"How did it go?" I asked, relieved that at least she was alive.

"Oh, Mr. Smith," she said, "we had one dreadful day."

I felt a chill. I hadn't been keen about six young women spending a weekend in that isolated house, miles of bad road from the nearest phone, the nearest doctor, the nearest policeman. The nearest help of any kind would be a mile away at Gomez's store.

Romulo Gomez is our landlord. He built our house, which stands on the cliffs above Santo Thomas Bay among nine other scattered houses. The spartan fisherman's port is three miles to the north, on a rocky point. There is no electricity.

"What happened, Mr. Smith," she said, "was really terrible! Miracle got bit by a rattlesnake!"

My heart stopped.

"Who?" I said weakly, feeling the perspiration. Could Miracle be one of her friends?

"Miracle," she said, "is the name of the dog."

85

I told her I didn't have time to listen to a dog story over the phone. We were going to her house that evening for dinner, and I could hear it then.

When she opened the door that evening, a strange dog was at her side. It wagged its tail and nuzzled my knee. It looked to me like a German shepherd pup, with maybe a touch of Doberman, six or seven months old. They already had two demented Dalmatians and didn't need a German shepherd.

"Whose dog?" I asked my son.

He spread his hands in resignation. "It's out of my control."

I cannot repeat Jacqueline's story verbatim. She talks rapidly, standing up, with many gestures and emotional interjections, and her French accent is not easily rendered into English.

But this is what happened.

The six women reached the house safely in the van. The next morning they drove the three miles over the rough road to the port, which is nothing more than a few squalid fishermen's shacks and a cantina that is sometimes open for beer. They hoped to buy some fish from a fisherman.

At the port the dog fell in with them, and they thought she was adorable and made a fuss over her. This was pretty heady stuff for a dog that had probably never known any human touch but the back of a fisherman's hand. Naturally, when they left, he tried to follow the van, but they left him in their dust, uttering cries, I suppose, of love and regret.

The next day they went back to the port on foot. The dog ran out to meet them, and this time she followed them all the way back to the house.

Just before they reached the house, though, when the dog was walking at my daughter-in-law's side, he was bitten by the rattlesnake. Of course it happened in a flash, but she insists she saw the snake strike out of a bush beside the road.

"How Is the Snake?"

"The snake jumped up out of the bushes, and he bit the poor dog right here," she said, clutching at her face near the mouth and staggering.

"What did you do?"

They had all begun picking up large rocks and hurling them down into the mesquite, hoping to kill the snake. They could hear him rattling furiously.

Then they drove the dog back to the port and took him to the fisherman who had seemed to be his owner.

"Can you believe it, Mr. Smith?" she said. "He did not care about z'dog. He said if a snake bit him he would die. He said it was good because he got the chickens."

They drove the dog to Gomez's store. A good idea. At La Bocana, as his place is known, Gomez is next to God.

"You know what Gomez said?" she demanded, as if finished with him forever. He said, "How is the snake?"

It sounded like Gomez. Not a man to be easily perturbed.

They took the dog into the house, and that night her face began to swell horribly; and her eyes went vacant. She tried to demonstrate, puffing out her cheeks and making her eyes go vacant. It was horrible.

When they were ready for bed, the dog was prostrate, evidently unconscious and dying. She couldn't stand it. The women were weeping and praying. She wanted to put the dog outside on the porch, because she couldn't stand the thought of her dying in the house while she slept. But another of the women couldn't stand to see her shut out.

"Mr. Smith, she take her pillow and lay down right by the dog and go to sleep!"

In the morning, when my daughter-in-law woke up, the dog was standing by her bed, looking down into her face. The swelling had subsided. The dog was alert; she had made it.

88   "Mr. Smith, right that minute we knew what to call her
—Miracle!"

Having worked a miracle, or at least witnessed one, they
could not simply wash their hands of it. They could not
leave the dog in Baja, where people cared more about the
snake.

On the way home they found a "gringo" veterinarian in
Ensenada. He gave the dog a rabies shot and said she would
live. For the certificate necessary to take the dog across the
border, they gave her name as Samantha. Their thinking in
that was subtle beyond belief. They feared that if they told
the customs agents the dog's name was Miracle they might
become suspicious that there was something extraordinary
about her and not allow her to cross into the United States.
The customs agent didn't even ask to see her certificate.

At dinner that evening the dog came over and sat beside
my chair, her muzzle at my knee.

"That might be the dog you've always wanted," my wife
said.

"No way," I said. "I've had my last dog."

Anyway, I thought, I certainly wouldn't want a dog
named Miracle.

I'd call her Samantha.

I Was in Trouble

A week or so later the dog was in my backyard along with
my wife's aged Yorkie, Fluff. Fluff, I had promised myself,
was the last dog we were ever going to have.

It grew upon me that I had been ensnared in a mon-
strous conspiracy. I sensed that the net had been prepared
for me from the beginning and that even my wife was in on
it.

Jacqueline and our son and their two children had come
by on their way for a week's vacation at Mammoth Lakes.
She had asked if we could keep the dog while they were

gone, and being faced with the reality of her on my door-step, I said okay, for one week only.

They came through the front door. The dog was not on a leash. She bounded about the house, skidding rugs out of place, knocking over vases and trashing magazines. I had forgotten what a large puppy was like. I took her by the collar and manhandled her through the kitchen door into the backyard.

"Oh, Mr. Smith," my daughter-in-law said anxiously. "I must tell you—she is an inside dog."

Incredible. They'd had her a week and already she was an inside dog—a dog that had never known anything but sand and cactus and the moon. If she had ever been inside at all, it would have been the inside of a fisherman's shack, and most likely she would have been kicked out.

"Is she housebroken?" I asked.

"Not yet."

"While she's here," I said, "she's an outside dog."

The dog had loped out into the backyard and was bouncing about, exploring. My granddaughter ran after her.

"Here, Miracle!" she cried.

I couldn't stand that name. If she wanted to be fed by me, she would have to answer to Samantha. I got a pan and put a scoop of kibbles in it, thinking the best way to accustom a dog to a new yard was to feed it.

"Mr. Smith," my daughter-in-law said. "Miracle does not like dog food."

"Oh?" I said. "What does she like?"

"Oh, you know. Vegetables, meat . . ."

"Today," my son said, simply offering it as a fact, "she gave her a pork chop."

"Here," I said, "she gets dog food."

"But Mr. Smith," my daughter-in-law protested, "I'm afraid she will not eat it. She will starve!"

I set the pan of kibbles in the patio, and the dog ran up and sniffed at it. She turned away.

"You see," my daughter-in-law said.

"Give her a couple of days," I said.

90   We sat on the patio a while and watched the two dogs size each other up.

"Mr. Smith," my daughter-in-law said, "you see—they are going to be good friends."

"Not that it matters," I said. Miracle was going back at the end of the week.

"I don't think you understand," my son said quietly, "what's happening to you."

I looked at my wife. She was noncommittal. If she had turned on me, I was in trouble.

I Thought of Her as Temporary

The next morning my daughter-in-law Gail phoned, cheerful as usual. "Hi," she said, "I just wondered how you were getting along."

"I'm all right," I said, wondering why she had called to ask, especially.

"I mean you and the dog," she said.

So she was in on it, too. Like Jacqueline, she already had two dogs and probably knew her husband wouldn't want one more.

It was becoming clear to me. They had got together on it and agreed that the best place for the dog they regarded as the product of a miracle was my backyard. And my own wife, as I had suspected, was in on it, working from within. What treachery!

Two weeks later, we still had the dog. By then she was eating dog food, and she answered to Samantha. Despite her collusion in the plot, my wife's patience was tried. Our multilevel pool area is ornamented with hundreds of potted plants, each of which my wife potted herself, and she couldn't help showing her irritation every morning when she looked out the window and saw the daily toll. Samantha knocked pots over like bowling pins.

She also got hold of my swimming trunks, which she

merely worried rather than shredded; she tossed pool towels about with the frenzy of a bull tossing a matador's cape; and she dug at the roots of the butterfly bush my wife had planted by the pool.

I rather enjoyed all this. I had predicted it, remembering the months of destruction brought down on us by the Airedale before he grew sedate and respectful of property.

I couldn't help liking Sam. She was glossy black, with tan markings. Her ears hadn't been trained, so they flopped. And the traces of the rattlesnake bite still showed on her lip. I had no doubt that that's what it was. She made me think that she had not lived through that ordeal only to be cast out on the street.

When I took my daily swim, she would trot down to the pool and run along beside me so that she would meet me when I reached the other end. No one else had ever shown that much interest in my rehabilitation.

I remember looking out the kitchen window and seeing her on the patio with Fluff just before I left the house that morning she got away. My wife had already driven off to work. I came home in midafternoon. I looked out the window and didn't see her; and somehow I was afraid right then that she was gone. We have a big fenced yard; she could have been many places out of my sight. But when I opened the door she didn't come.

Only at that moment did I realize how much I had begun to like her. I felt dejected and guilty, though I told myself it wasn't my fault. I walked around the fence. All four gates were secure. Maybe someone had come into the yard and inadvertently left a gate open long enough for her to get out. Maybe she had squirmed under the fence. Maybe someone had stolen her.

I drove up and down the hill, looking. We had caught the Airedale often enough. But he knew where he was. He never went far, and if we didn't find him, he would come home. I was afraid that Sam, once she got away, would never find her way back.

92 I didn't see her. In a way that was good. She wasn't dead in the street. She wouldn't be very savvy about cars.

The next morning I went to the Ann Street Animal Shelter to see if she had turned up there. It was not heartening. I walked up and down the aisles, looking into the cages of the derelicts from the streets.

How different they were! Not just in looks, in which they ranged from miniatures to giant working dogs, but in personality. Some were still puppies, awkward and appealing; some were friendly, good-natured tail waggers; some were frighteningly hostile, thrusting heads from massive shoulders, baring fangs, growling, barking as if insane.

Others—many of them—seemed disconnected, unaware, staring off into some forgotten distance; perhaps psychotic.

Samantha was not there.

Every day for three days one or the other of us went down to the shelter; but Samantha never turned up. We ran a classified ad in the paper for four days and got some calls. Most of them were from far afield, and the wrong dog. A brindle dog in West Los Angeles. A spaniel in Glendale. A woman drove up to the house with a dog in the front seat. Wasn't even close.

Then we got some news that was momentarily encouraging. A woman down our street had taken the dog in, not knowing she was ours. She liked her and was going to keep her, but it just happened that her own dog was wearing a cast for a broken bone, and she couldn't have another dog in the yard with him—especially not a big, gawky, playful dog like Sam. She fed Sam and hoped she'd stay, but Sam disappeared.

So we knew she'd been around. She hadn't been hit by a car or stolen—at least not for the first two days.

It was a false hope. We had no further trace.

My daughter-in-law forgave me, but I doubt that she will ever trust me with one of her dogs again. My record is poor.

Over the years I have kept three dogs for them when

they went on vacation. The first was a big black Labrador. I thought it would be a good time to have him neutered, while they were gone, and asked their permission. They agreed. He died on the operating table.

The second dog was also a Labrador, chocolate colored; they called him Choco. He was big, amiable, lazy, and naturally overweight. My daughter-in-law fed him tasty table scraps. He fell ill while he was in my care and was ill when they returned and took him home. He never recovered. He was dead in a week.

And then Samantha.

I know that if we'd had a tag made for her with our telephone number on it we'd probably have got her back.

But I thought of her as so temporary.

THE WAY WE WERE

Software Wasn't Even a Word

A reader who knows my vintage, evidently, has sent me an extraordinary article from the *Wellesley* magazine (first printed in the *Boston Globe)* by Nardi Reeder Campion, Wellesley, 1938.

It impressed and dazzled me, and I doubt that a Yale or a Harvard or even a Princeton man could have done it.

It is simply called "1938," and it is an inventory of the things the class of 1938 did not have—had never heard of—that are everyday realities today.

Unfortunately, since I regard plagiarism as the major sin available to me, I can not simply reprint the entire article, as I would like to do, but the first paragraph should give you the idea:

We were before television. Before penicillin, polio shots, antibiotics, and Frisbees. Before frozen food, nylon, Dacron, Xerox, Kinsey. We were before radar, fluorescent lights, credit cards and ballpoint pens. For us, time-sharing meant togetherness, not computers; a chip meant a piece of wood; hardware meant hardware; and software wasn't even a word. . . .

95

Take each of those items and imagine how your life
might be different without it.

Penicillin. I don't know about you, but *I'd* probably be
dead. That pneumonia in 1982 might well have taken me
off.

Polio shots. Summers indeed were long and hot for the
parents of small children before the vaccines.

Antibiotics. They saved me this year.

Frisbees. I don't think my life would have been any the
less gratifying if there had been no Frisbees, but I do remember how delighted I was to look out the window of our
hotel in Cambridge, England, and see two youths throwing
a Frisbee on the green, knowing that this pretty sport had
come to one of the English-speaking world's most storied
cultural centers from the inventive ferment of our own Los
Angeles.

Frozen foods. No need to talk about it.

Nylon, Dacron. I know they have their uses, but there
was something exotic and seductive about silk stockings,
and the very word *silk* has never been equaled by the word
for anything synthetic.

Xerox. Without it I would never have had a copy of
Campion's article.

Kinsey. If all that stuff was going on, why did everyone
pretend to be so surprised when he told us it was? Kinsey
did not prove that sex existed in America; he just made it
fashionable to talk about it.

No use going on with the rest of them. There's no end to
this. It seems incredible that all those things have come into
our lives since Campion's class graduated. But that was only
her first paragraph. At the risk of exceeding the amount I
can quote without her permission, I will give you one more
paragraph:

We were before Batman, 'Grapes of Wrath,' Ru-
dolph the Rednosed Reindeer, 'Stuart Little,' and
Snoopy. Before DDT and vitamin pills, vodka (in
the United States) and the white wine craze, dispos-

able diapers, Q.E. One, jeeps, the Jefferson memorial and the Jefferson nickel. . . . Before Scotch tape, Grand Coulee Dam, Paine, Webber, Merrill, Lynch; M and M's, the automatic shift and Lincoln Continentals . . .

It makes me wonder. If we didn't have DDT, we probably didn't have Black Flag. How did we kill our bugs? I had forgotten all about bugs. Memory has that benign effect: One forgets the trivial irritations.

I do remember some bedbugs in Denver. When I was on the road in the Depression, I got a room in Denver one night for fifteen cents, and when I awoke the next morning, I was polka-dotted with bites. That couldn't happen today. You can't find a hotel room, even in Denver, for fifteen cents.

I could get along today quite well without vodka, though my wife likes a vodka tonic when she comes home from work, but I don't know how we'd get through dinner without our white wine. Of course, white wine was *known* back in the cultural dark ages of the 1930s, but my own parents were too uncivilized to have discovered it. My father learned to drink whatever he could get from his bootlegger during Prohibition and had no taste at all for wine.

I could certainly get along without Paine, Webber, Merrill, and Lynch and Lincoln Continentals, and even the automatic shift, though I am more and more reconciled to it as time goes by. It might be hard, though, to keep everything together without Scotch tape.

You might think those two paragraphs had just about exhausted the possibilities. That's what I thought. I thought the rest of her article would be taken up with philosophizing over the items she had already listed.

Not so. The article goes on for two more pages—paragraph after paragraph packed tight with things that Nardi Reeder and her classmates were "before."

As I scanned the rest, one line—stunning in its implications—stood out: "We were before pantyhose. . . ."

98 Now do you sense the primitive world she is really describing?

Finally, she recalls that they did have one thing we don't have today—humorists who were funny—Thurber, Benchley, E. B. White, Charlie Chaplin, Bea Lillie, W. C. Fields, Ogden Nash, the Marx Brothers.

"Who could forget Groucho as Dr. Quackinbush taking a pulse and saying, 'Either this man is dead or my watch has stopped.'?"

"Quick, Henry, the Flit!"

Perhaps it's just as well that I quoted only two paragraphs from Nardi Reeder Campion's *Wellesley* magazine article on the wonders of the twentieth century that hadn't yet appeared when she and her classmates graduated in 1938.

Just those two paragraphs—and especially my amplifications—have raised enough dispute.

My worst assumption came from her recollection that the girls of 1938 didn't have DDT.

I am embarrassed by a number of brief but well-aimed missives, including this postcard from Rex D. Walker, physics teacher at John Marshall High School. It says: "How did we kill our bugs? Henry knew!"

Steve R. Riskin, a lawyer in Venice, is more specific: "Don't you remember? 'Quick, Henry, the Flit!' "

Of course. How could I have forgotten one of the most popular advertising slogans of the 1930s?

It not only was the distress call sounded when a bug threatened to disrupt a picnic or perhaps a romantic clinch, but it was taken into the language as a call for help in any minor emergency.

Donna Byrd reminds us that Flit came in a spray can—not aerosol—and we directed it against the enemy by pushing the plunger. By the way, she says, "The fellow that drew

Henry didn't fade away with Flit—he's better known as Dr. Seuss."

Also, I was mistaken, evidently, in thinking that we didn't have Black Flag before 1938.

"During the '30s," writes Bill McCormick of Garden Grove, "I worked in a neighborhood hardware store ($15 per week) and we carried a line of Black Flag insecticides. The list of active agents included such things as pyrethrin and nicotine."

Robert E. Johnson of West Hollywood was a "callow youth" on a farm in the 1930s and used Black Flag on the chicken coop. "It was a noxious black liquid which consisted of extract of tobacco containing a high concentration of nicotine—as witness Black Flag's logo of the time, a tobacco leaf on a black flag. . . ."

Not very romantic, I concede, but no error is too trivial to deserve correction.

Not I, but Campion herself seems to have erred in listing Scotch tape as not existing yet in 1938.

"On Jan. 1, 1937," writes Jean Otis Reinecke of Reinecke Associates, industrial designers, Flintridge, "I *re*-designed the first Scotch brand tape dispenser, and, so far as I know, have designed every one since. . . ."

Joseph N. Ingham quotes the 1930 annual report of the Minnesota Mining and Manufacturing Co. "During the year a new product known as Scotch Brand Cellophane tape was introduced."

An error of graver consequence is imputed to me for a paragraph I wrote about the Frisbee, which Campion listed among the joys of our century that the Wellesley girls of 1938 were "before."

Writes Bobby Ramsen: "The Frisbee, sir, was 'invented' by Yale students in New Haven, Conn., who took to throwing tin pie plates to each other in the early 1950s. The name 'Frisbee Baking Co.' was embossed on the bottom of each tin plate."

I would simply concede this point if we were not dealing here with an important bit of cultural history. I have writ-

ten about the origins of the Frisbee before, and in my file is a 1978 letter from Dr. Robert K. Woods, then director of the Institute of Frisbee Medicine, Santa Monica. Dr. Woods noted that the Yale story was a "popular theory" but cited evidence that it was the lid of a Frisbie cookie tin, not a pie tin, that was tossed, and it was at Harvard, not Yale, that the term "Frisbie-ing" was first heard by Rick Knerr, cofounder of Wham-O, the San Gabriel company that manufactures Frisbees.

It was Fred Morrison, though, who first sold pie tins on Southern California beaches after World War II and quickly saw the advantage of a durable, aerodynamically stable, lightweight, and *quiet* saucer made of plastic.

Thus, in the inventive ferment of our own Los Angeles . . .

My memory of Cambridge brings back a similar experience to Virginia Petersen. She writes,

> I, too, recall with unforgettable delight a Frisbee scene outside the then largest hotel in the world, the Rossiya in Moscow. We were preparing to board our buses for the Moscow airport—deep snow on the ground and more falling heavily—hundreds of dour-faced Russians rushing in and out of the huge double doors of the hotel—and several of our young Oberlin students joyously tossing a Frisbee high above the main entrance of the hotel to the utter astonishment of every Russian. Such exuberant and frivolous spontaneity was totally beyond their ken . . . a beautiful sight!

Sydney S. Fast, UCLA, 1937, reminds us that we haven't seen everything yet.

> I am reminded of my once vigorous father (Stanford 1911) who was dying of cancer in the fall of 1969. He was so enthusiastic about the many scientific and other discoveries in his lifetime that he'd 'be

damned' if he would die before they put a man on the moon. . . . What wonders will there be in our children's postgraduate years?

God knows; but nothing, I trust, to match the three *P*'s —Penicillin, the Pill, and Pantyhose.

There Was Nothing Wrong with My Body

It was a date I never expected to see. To young people, it seems as improbably far in the future as science fiction. But if you live long enough, it comes.

In July I went to my 1934 class reunion on the fiftieth anniversary of our graduation from Belmont High School, which stands today exactly one mile west of my office in the *Times.* My orbit had been small.

Oddly, it is not as grim a rite as it sounds. After half a century in what we once looked forward to as "the real world," we have banked most of our fires; our passions are subdued; our regrets blurred, our demons exorcised. We are rather surprised to be here at all, and not entirely discontented.

We picnicked at Point Fermin Park, down near the harbor lighthouse, under clumps of eucalyptus trees, cooled by a light breeze off San Pedro Channel, while the rest of the city sweltered. We had decided that some of our classmates might not be able to afford a restaurant. If you went through high school in the central city in the Great Depression, you never forgot it.

Besides, we always loved the beach, because we knew, in the words of one of our songs, that the best things in life are free.

We marked our own name tags, women writing in their

102 maiden names in case the maiden name should ring some distant bell. Ah, my bells did ring a time or two.

Persons who hadn't gone to Belmont but had married a member of our class identified themselves by their spouses' names. Thus, I was astonished to see that Barry Bertram had printed that name on his tag but added Mr. Minnie Bornstein.

Everybody in the class knew Minnie, who was among our best, brightest, and most buoyant. Like most of us, she didn't have the money for college; but years later, after raising a family, she went to law school. Her tag said Minnie Bornstein, and in parentheses, Manya Bertram—her married name and the one she uses in her practice of the law.

We didn't have a potato-sack race or play baseball. We just talked. People with common interests would drift together.

"Welcome to the club," Dick McKeon said heartily to me, reaching across a basket of fried chicken to shake my hand. I didn't know what he meant for a moment. Dick had been our student-body president, a hard-driving achiever who had emerged suddenly from obscurity to dominate the campus.

He ran an index finger in a straight line down his chest, and I realized he meant to welcome me to the heart-bypass club.

I happened to be sitting on the bench beside another member, Jerry Luboviski, retired as advertising director and a vice-president of Union Oil. Another classmate, Carl Hartnack, who had gone from Belmont directly into an eighteen-dollar-a-week job at Security (now Pacific) First National, had risen to president and then chairman of the board, and when he put up the bank's new tower in the downtown skyline, it was designed so his office looked down on the Belmont playing field.

I wondered if Carl was a member of the bypass club yet. We hadn't been a laid-back generation.

The reunion to avoid, it seems to me, is not the fiftieth but the twenty-fifth. That is the trap. It catches everyone at mid-life crisis. It throws vulnerable people together in a kind of brutal encounter at a moment when they are already abraded by regrets, bewildered by uncertainties, and tormented by resurgent fantasies.

Women are anxious about menopause and fading beauty, about empty homes and errant husbands; men look in the mirror and no longer see Charles Boyer or Charles Atlas. Jealousies are sharpened; spouses measure their mates against the ones that got away; infidelity is contemplated, if not accomplished; and almost everyone goes home vaguely disenchanted.

By the way, I attended two fiftieth anniversaries that year. One was the fiftieth of the Whittier Union High School class of 1934. I attended Whittier throughout my freshman year and in fact was class president.

The reunion was held in April, before my surgery, at the Hacienda Heights Country Club, and was made especially memorable for me by the total recall of one of our brightest classmates—Dorothy Welch. (Dorothy had not only been clearly my scholastic superior at John Muir Junior High and in that freshman high school year, but she was also one of the two girls who could beat me in the seventy-five-yard dash.)

In a brief talk she made at the reunion, Dorothy recalled that when I made my first speech as class president I was "very nervous," and she confessed that she had once conceived of her ideal as a boy with "Ed Smith's body and Jack Smith's mind." (Ed Smith was there that night. He still looked somewhat like Adonis, if you care for the type, including those blond ringlets.)

I asked Dorothy how she could remember such details after fifty years, and she said she had put them down in her diary.

I'd never had a hint from her that she felt that way about me, and it's a good thing she didn't let it out at our twenty-fifth reunion. That would have caught me in mid-life crisis, and I might have responded in some foolish way.

104

No. Playboy, No. Penthouse

I took my oldest grandson to a shoe store the other day to buy him a pair of shoes for his fifteenth birthday.

He picked out a pair of Adidas that cost $52.23.

A top-quality pair of tennis shoes when I was fifteen might have cost four dollars.

But the price didn't surprise me. In 1931, when people with good jobs earned twenty-five dollars a week, four dollars for a pair of shoes was dearer than fifty-two dollars is today.

I was thinking about what a different world altogether it is for a fifteen-year-old boy these days.

We had our own music, too, as the young today have rock and its multitude of gods and goddesses. We had grown up with jazz, and Rudy Vallee had introduced "crooning," and Bing Crosby had just burst on society as its prime exponent.

Of course, we were not so divided from our parents by music as the younger generation is today, and has been for twenty years; our mothers loved Rudy, too, even if our fathers didn't.

We were not rabid, as today's young music lovers seem to be; we were moony. We believed that she might not be an angel, but still she'd do; we believed two souls were mated the day she came along; we believed in dancing cheek to cheek. Today's messages are more graphic and perhaps more realistic.

It was the year I learned to drive. A business partner of my father's, a man who owned a maroon Franklin sedan, let me drive it one day, in town, cold plunge. It was *the* American rite of passage. I was a man.

Of course, my attitude toward women was perfectly expressed by the lyrics Bing sang, and it was to stay that way for several years. In my senior year, when I took a girl to the prom, the band played "Good Night, Lovely Little

Lady," and I sang it in her ear as we danced. That's as far as it went.

I didn't drink. I didn't smoke. And it was impossible for me to be in love with any ordinary mortal, because I was in love with Clara Bow, Claudette Colbert, Helen Twelvetrees, and Madeleine Carroll. Hoover was president, and there didn't seem any hope of rising out of the Depression; but nobody worried about annihilation.

I had seen Pat O'Brien as Hildy Johnson in *The Front Page,* and I knew what I wanted to be: a hardworking, fast-talking newspaper reporter whose job was more important to him than his fiancée. Since I had no fiancée and no job, I was not called upon to make that choice. In later years, however, it came up.

Since there was no television and movies cost a quarter, I spent a lot of my time after school at the public library. I had no guidance in what I read (it was rarely related to schoolwork), so I just drifted through the stacks, one book leading to another, and got a rather spotty education.

The teen years are hard for boys. I suppose they're hard for girls, too; but all I know about is boys. Gradually you have to give up your childhood fantasies. You aren't going to run the 100 meters in the Olympic Games. You aren't going to play second base for the Hollywood Stars, much less the New York Yankees. Maybe you aren't even going to get a job on a newspaper. And surely you are never going to hold that walking, talking dream in your arms.

Of course, these days teenagers have all those teen-sex movies to guide them through their frustrations. Intimate relationships that I had to infer from the unimpassioned kisses of William Powell and Carole Lombard are demonstrated in the nude, or nearly so. The Hollywood Code kept us from ever seeing even a married couple in the same bed, much less in conjugal embrace.

We had no *Playboy* or *Penthouse* magazines to picture in intimate detail, and in ecstatic color, that object of our fevered imaginations, the female anatomy divine. One of the things I used to read at the library was the *National*

106 *Geographic* because of all the bare breasts one found in it, even though they were all in Borneo, Bora-Bora, or New Guinea.

Somehow I also discovered Somerset Maugham, and he awakened me, in *Of Human Bondage*, to the disappointments and ironies of manhood; and Thomas Wolfe (that's not Tom Wolfe), who introduced me to the poetry of life in America.

I wish my grandson well in his new shoes.

You Ever Heard of the Beatles?

From time to time I am depressed when I mention Iwo Jima to some teenager or yuppie and he says, "Iwo Jima? What's that?"

It seemed terribly important at the time. Nearly 7,000 young American men died to wrest that island from the Japanese in World War II, and 22,000 Japanese were shot, blown up, or burned alive in their caves.

I have always accepted the American justification for that carnage. It was said that we needed the island for our bombers to make emergency landings on after their runs over Tokyo. In fact, I saw the first B-29 land—of the hundreds that were to land there before the war ended.

Tokyo was being devastated by incendiary raids; the war seemed all but over, and yet the Japanese fought on tenaciously. To bring them to their knees we A-bombed Hiroshima.

Does anyone ask, "What's Hiroshima?" I wouldn't be surprised. How quickly past events vanish from our own time frame into the fold of history.

History today is a series of swift chain reactions, speeded up like a Keystone Kops movie by instant revelation on radio and television. In the days of the American Revolution it took weeks for news of one event to travel between the colonies and England and weeks for the reaction to take place. Today we bomb Libya and two minutes later the whole world knows it.

In earlier centuries people could live out their lives without being aware of any changes in the order of things. A king might die; the tides of war might sweep over their towns and pastures; but nothing much changed.

What made me think a teenager would know of Iwo Jima? It was already twenty years into history when today's twenty-one-year-old was born. To a small boy playing at war—do they still do that?—Iwo Jima today is only twenty years from being as far away as the Civil War was to me when I was a small boy.

I still remember veterans of the Civil War tottering down Bakersfield's melting streets on the Fourth of July, Yankees and Confederates together in their faded uniforms. The last Civil War veteran died in 1959.

Even the last of the Spanish-American War veterans may be about to go. *Times* writer Bill Murphy reported in February 1986 that only nine who answered President McKinley's call for volunteers in 1898 were left. According to the Veterans Administration, as of January, 1989, only one remained alive.

The ranks of World War I's doughboys are growing thin, and few will live out the century. To be realistic I must point out also that before we are very far into the next century, all the veterans of World War II will be gone, too. Every last man and woman of us.

I am always bemused when I see photographs of distinguished business tycoons of the late nineteenth century seated around tables at some civic banquet with their beards against their glaring shirtfronts and I realize that they are all quite dead; or when I see a photograph of men, women, and children playing in the surf at the beach in their modest swimsuits in front of one of those wonderful old Victorian pavilions.

Recently Timothy P. Merrigan, aged thirty-one, wrote that I am far behind the time in my shock at finding Iwo Jima forgotten.

108   "True melancholy," he said, "is mentioning The Beatles to a teen-ager and getting the response, 'Who are they?' Or Watergate. And being informed that he'd just read about it in his history book?"

Watergate is *history* already? Of course it is, and so are Joe McCarthy and Ike and Truman and MacArthur and Babe Ruth and Elvis.

Does *anyone* remember Roger Bannister?

But I couldn't believe that anyone had never heard of the Beatles. It seemed just the other day that they burst upon the world with all that fresh young vigor, spontaneity, humor, heart, impudence, and talent.

Of course, the Beatles had long since broken up as a group, and one of them was dead at the hand of a madman. The remaining three had gone their separate ways; but surely there was no one living who didn't remember them or didn't know who they were and how they turned the world of youth into a kind of joyous madness in the early 1960s with "Love Me Do" and "I Want To Hold Your Hand."

I decided I had to find out. I telephoned my granddaughter Alison, who had just turned nine.

"Have you ever heard of the Beatles?" I asked her.

"Yes," she said.

"Who were they."

She didn't hesitate. "They were old singers, and whenever they sang, girls came up screaming."

Old? The Beatles old?

Well, Ringo Starr is almost forty-six. But don't worry. At least some of us will still love them when they're sixty-four.

My Father Taught Me
Pool, Poker, and H. L. Mencken

My Hollywood correspondent, Duke Russell, who has his philosophical moods, writes to comment on a recent report of mine on High School Night at the Philharmonic.

"It brought back great memories of Hollywood High," he says, "where we were all required to take a class called Music and Art Appreciation. Ten weeks of listening to classical music. Ten weeks of learning about art.

"I was not exactly an honor student. I was interested in baseball and basketball and the beach. But of all the classes I took, music appreciation was one of the highlights. Chopin, Mozart, Rossini, Tchaikovsky, Beethoven, and many others entered my pool hall life and have been my good friends ever since. . . ."

I, too, remember music and art appreciation and have been forever grateful for those two required classes that seemed so onerous to most pupils at the time.

I took them at Belmont High School in the early 1930s. I was living then in an apartment house on Ingraham. It had a billiard room that was much classier than a mere plebeian pool hall. Only elderly gentlemen whose worst vice was smoking cigars played there, but I spent most of my evenings shooting pool in that mahagony-paneled room when I should have been upstairs studying. My father taught me three things: pool, poker, and H. L. Mencken. He considered them fundamental to any young man's education.

At school, I, too, was most interested in basketball, and I remember with what reluctance I dragged myself once a week to the classroom where a teacher whose name I no longer remember was supposed to teach us an appreciation of art and music.

We had radios at home, and occasionally I heard opera;

110   but mostly it was prizefights, football games, Jack Benny, and "Amos 'n' Andy."

Adolescents did not then own expensive stereo equipment and cabinets filled with tapes and records. Nor did expensive art books decorate every cocktail table.

I knew nothing of Mozart or Michelangelo.

But to this day, like Russell, when I hear Chopin, Mozart, Rossini, Tchaikovsky, or Beethoven, my mind drifts back to those warm afternoons in the classroom when the teacher sat immobile beside the school's precious windup Victrola, watching our faces hopefully for some light of response, while the voice of the great Caruso, thin, scratchy, tinny, and remote, but still magnificent, came out of the walnut box. It might be "La Donna è Mobile" or "O Sòle Mio," both of which came to represent grand opera for me.

I also will never forget the "Anvil Chorus" from Verdi's *Il Trovatore*. How I loved all those people singing at the tops of their lungs while the blacksmith kept the beat by banging on his anvil. What a song!

I also learned to appreciate the thrilling cadenzas of the sopranos. I don't know who they were now. Probably Tebaldi and Galli-Curci, or maybe Lily Pons, but I loved the way their voices rose and fell, sweeter than any other sound I knew.

Whether the teacher anticipated my taste or whether she caused it to be what it is, I cannot today hear the quartet from *Rigoletto* or the sextet from *Lucia di Lammermoor* without feeling once more those thrills running up and down my spine as they did in that schoolroom.

Throw in a few Strauss waltzes, something from *The Marriage of Figaro*, and the "Triumphal March" from *Aida* and you will have a pretty good idea of my musical foundations.

Of course, we never let on to the teacher that we actually appreciated that music. If you were the first-string center on the class B basketball team, you didn't let on that you liked classical music, except for letting go in the locker room now and then with a chorus of "O Sòle Mio," which

was always rendered with heavy mock bravado (and in the
original Italian, or my best imitation of it).

So I don't know whether that poor teacher ever knew
that she really was teaching music appreciation just by dog-
gedly playing those records over and over again while her
pupils either went to sleep or passed notes to each other or
engaged in that most blissful of classroom activities—day-
dreaming.

To this day, when I'm at the Hollywood Bowl or the
Music Center listening to the symphony, I have a tendency
to drift off in daydreams. I wonder if that's conditioned by
my music appreciation class.

I don't have as vivid a memory of my art appreciation
class, but I do remember that it was regarded as a drag, like
music appreciation, and we took it only because we had to.

I don't believe we ever even made a trip to the museum
to see whatever art it then had, but we did see pictures of
such classics as Michelangelo's *David* and Whistler's mother
and even some contemporaries such as Picasso, so that
later, when I was invited to a cocktail party and was asked
by some sophisticated older college girl whether I was familiar with the work of Picasso, I could say, "Oh, yes—isn't he
the one who paints those two-faced women?"

Sometimes today I wonder how much of my small talk
about art and music at cocktail parties derives straight from
those old art and music appreciation classes and that
teacher who did her best, hoping that some of it might
stick.

I urge high school students not to scorn those classes;
they may be learning in them all they'll ever know about art
and music.

112

I Looked Like an Overaged Punk Rocker

Not long ago I received the following publicity handout:

> Back in the early sixties, when the Beatles had just emerged on the American record charts, Richard Stanley, then 20, put men and women in the same barber's chair.
>
> Stanley invented the first unisex hair salon . . . which changed the hair industry and was one of the greatest reasons why you don't see too many barber poles today. . . .

Unisex can be fun, and I am not hostile to the intrusion of women into most of the old male strongholds, like the saloon, the steam bath, and the pool hall.

But when it comes to barbershops, I'm still a sexist. There are beauty shops, and there are barbershops, and never the twain shall meet.

I happen to have an old-fashioned barber named Rudy. He has a one-man shop in Highland Park. I passed it one day and stopped in and asked him if he was a hair stylist.

"No," he said. "I'm a barber."

"That's what I'm looking for," I said. I've been with him ever since.

Rudy's reading material includes the *Times* and *Sports Illustrated,* of which he has not only the latest issue but also a stack of dog-eared back numbers.

There is usually a line of two or three men waiting in chairs, reading the paper or *SI* and talking about the Dodgers or the Angels or whatever is happening in sports.

I have seen women in the shop, but usually they have come in with small boys in tow, to offer them up to this male ritual. For a small boy, a haircut in a man's barbershop is a rite of passage.

When I was a boy, the barbershop was the most all male place in town. It reeked of hair oil and face lotion, masculine smells unlike the seductive aromas of the beauty shop or the woman's hair salon. Men read *Liberty* and *Collier's* and talked easily of Babe Ruth and Jack Dempsey and the government, which of course was going to hell.

In the summertime the barbershop was warm and intimate, with an electric fan raking the row of waiting men and stirring up the overladen air, and in October the barber's tinny radio carried the World Series; the announcer tried to give excitement to the action, which he was reading off the telegraph, play by play.

When you got in the chair, the barber's scissors made a clicking sound as he began his snipping, and you watched the progress of his artistry in one of those mirrors that reflected a mirror on the other side of the shop, back and forth into infinity.

When you were old enough and rich enough to have a shave, it was pure bliss, lying supine in the extended chair with the warm lather on your face, listening to the scrape of the razor as the barber made his delicate strokes.

One day a year or so ago, when my barber was on vacation, I decided to try a unisex salon in one of the shopping centers. I walked in and was directed to a chair by a hostess. Finally, a young woman came to fetch me and asked me what my name was. I told her it was Jack Smith.

"Okay, Jack," she said. "Just come with me."

She led me first to a large basin and put a towel around my shoulders.

"You have to have a shampoo first," she said.

I told her I didn't need a shampoo. I had had one that morning.

"You have to," she said. "It's a rule."

She gave me a shampoo and then led me to a chair in which I sat uneasily as she made a few theatrical snips at my wet hair.

All of a sudden she was finished. Obviously I was expected to tip her. I gave her two dollars, feeling cheap, and

114 put my jacket on and looked at myself in a mirror. I looked like an overaged punk rocker.

I went out to the cashier to pay my bill, which was more than double what I paid Rudy.

When Rudy came back, I stopped in to show him what I had done. "Don't worry, Jack," he said. "It'll grow out in a month or two."

As I say, unisex is a fine ideal, but let's keep those barber poles.

THE ANIMAL WORLD

Quiet Dogs, Monogamous Cats

I am alarmed as well as fascinated by the U.S. Patent and Trademark Office's decision to patent invented animals.

By invented animals they evidently mean new animal types, or perhaps new species, created by splicing genes. Producing new types through genetic manipulation is much faster than the old-fashioned method of selective breeding, which can take many generations.

At first glance this proposal seems innocent enough. Through genetic manipulation we can have cows that give more milk, sheep that bear more wool, dogs that don't bark, and so on.

But knowing human nature, we know that our biologists, once they get the green light, are not going to stop with simply increasing a cow's milk or making a thoroughbred horse run faster.

Man is an experimental creature and will do what he can do.

For centuries we have been breeding the jackass to the mare to produce the mule. And what do we have? An animal that is strong but stubborn beyond human endurance; and which, alas, is incapable of breeding with its own kind. The mule is a dead end.

Some zoos, I believe, have produced ligers by breeding

116   lions and tigers. This is an exotic animal that captures our
fancy, but if I'm not mistaken, ligers can not breed successfully, either.

I'm sure, however, that science will find a way around
this roadblock and that our new invented creatures will
soon be breeding away like rabbits. We will have to declare
open season on them so hunters can keep them under control, like mountain lions.

I suppose that in granting patents for invented animals
the Patent Office merely has its eye on the development of
salable products, all of which will contribute to the national
economy.

What if, for example, we were able to produce a cow
that gave light beer instead of milk? That would probably
revitalize the dairy industry and bring back good times to
all the farm states.

We who watch the beer ads during football games on
television would soon be regaled by commercials showing
buxom pink-cheeked beermaids squeezing pails filled with
foamy beer from contented cows.

Who knows but what some genius in the laboratory will
actually come up with an umbus, "a sort of cow" invented
by Dr. Seuss. If you remember, the umbus has one head and
one tail, like any ordinary cow, but—

*She has ninety-eight faucets that give milk quite nicely /
Perhaps ninety-nine / I forget just precisely.*

I suppose that would still be a cow, though an amazing
one indeed.

But inevitably some kinky biologist will want to go a
little further and create a new species. An individual
wouldn't have to be very much different from an existing
species to be declared a new one by the taxonomists, who
make up their own rules.

I wonder how the Patent Office will rule on such animals, if they should ever appear. What if some scientist,
tinkering with the genes of the camel, turns out a spazzim?

The spazzim, as every reader of Dr. Seuss knows, is a
kind of cross between a yak and a camel, except that he has

an arabesque set of antlers that travelers may use to hang up such articles as umbrellas, clocks, coffee cups, and grasshopper cages.

I doubt that the spazzim will ever replace the automobile, but it ought to be a welcome innovation in the lands of the nomads, if there are any left.

Would our unknown biologist get a patent for the spazzim, since he gave it life? Or would the patent belong to Dr. Seuss, who thought up the spazzim and brought him into being first, if only on paper?

I see all kinds of litigation arising from the awarding of patents for new species. "Dr. Seuss Sues to Protect Fuddle from Patent Infringement" . . . "Biologist Claims He Created the Yuzz," and so on.

But there are moral as well as practical uncertainties in this development.

Isn't it man's ultimate arrogance to encroach on God's exclusive right to create species?

Actually, God has done an astounding job. There are a million species of animal life on earth, each one different from the others, and in their variety they are even more improbable than the inventions of Dr. Seuss.

Has Dr. Seuss invented anything more wonderful than the kangaroo and the wallaby, who carry their children in a pouch; the trap-door spider, who builds a door to lure victims into his parlor; *Micromalthus debilis,* a tiny male fly that, after five days of life, devours its mother; the bat, the hippopotamus, the praying mantis, the penguin, the giraffe, the Monarch butterfly?

The Patent Office is not yet prepared to issue patents on human alterations. But sooner or later the biologists will begin trying to remake us. In 20,000 years of selective breeding we have not been able to eliminate the baboon in our nature. Why not try?

Meanwhile, I wish they'd take some smaller steps and just give us quiet dogs and monogamous cats.

I Never Knew a Moral Cat

Writing in the *Guardian*, Nicholas Humphrey wonders whether animals have the intelligence to deceive. As he puts it bluntly, "To tell lies."

He notes that researchers have discovered behavior in chimpanzees that suggests deceptive intent. For example, one chimpanzee will lead his fellows away from a cache of fruit, then come back and eat it all himself. A female will deceive the dominant male of her tribe to do some private grooming with another male she favors.

He also points out that a certain moth, when threatened by a bird, will spread its wings to display a pair of enormous, terrifying eyes. There is no doubt, he says, that the moth has acted to deceive. "He has issued a false message." But perhaps it has no intent to deceive, he suggests; its act is simply instinctive, though it has a favorable result.

Being no more a scientist than I am, Humphrey bases his own conclusion not on chimpanzees or insects but on his dog.

First he points out how he deceives his dog. Wanting to shut the dog in the house, he opens the door and rattles his pan in the kitchen. Expecting to be fed, the dog comes in. "I shut him in and leave."

It is quite clear in that case that Humphrey is deceiving his dog.

But suppose Humphrey is sitting in his easy chair. The dog scratches on the door as if he wants out. Humphrey gets up to open the door. The dog runs around him and jumps into the chair.

Has the dog not deliberately deceived him?

Humphrey observes that the answer is important because it can reveal so much about the level of an animal's imagination.

Like Humphrey, I have never been deceived by a chimpanzee, but I have many times been deceived by dogs, and even more times by cats. Cats are the most duplicitous of creatures and capable of the subtlest deception.

Have you ever watched a cat toy with a mouse? The cat crouches in his immemorial instinctive way. Rear legs drawn under his haunches in the best position to spring, front paws demurely extended. The mouse, four feet away, is terrified. It doesn't know whether to pretend that he doesn't exist or to make a dash for it.

The cat does not look at the mouse. Like the Sphinx itself, he looks bland, stony and uninterested. The mouse is deceived. He thinks the cat is not aware of him. Finally, it makes its move—a foolish dash for safety. The cat pounces, and in one leap has the mouse in his paws.

Then begins a series of cruel deceptions. The cat plays with the mouse. He lets it go. Evidently he couldn't care less. The mouse makes another tentative run for it. The cat makes one short hop and has the mouse in his paws again.

It is deceptive, deliberate, and despicable behavior, and I think the cat must answer for it.

As for confiscating their masters' chairs, cats are more duplicitous and adept than dogs. I have had numerous cats that loved my chair. They would hide quietly under a nearby table, waiting for me to get up for a moment; when I returned, the chair would be taken. I am positive that deception was a part of this strategy.

My Airedale, Fleetwood Pugsley, was Machiavellian in his duplicity. Many times when he escaped our yard, I would chase him down the hill, calling for him to come to me, his master. He would often trot toward me, head down as if in docile submission, only to wheel away, as I reached for his collar, and bound into a neighbor's yard.

I have never owned another dog that had so much ability to pretend he was interested in one thing, completely ignoring the thing he really had his mind on, only to switch directions and go after the prize when you thought his intentions were innocent.

Since he had been neutered, he was no trouble in this respect with female dogs, but if he saw an open door or an open gate, his pretense of ignoring it was fascinating to watch.

120   Pugsley's deceptions were not as exquisite or sinister as those of cats. He was more childlike. But I have no doubt that his behavior was deceptive; that he knew he was distracting or fooling me, with the deliberate intent of getting away with something forbidden.

What this means to me is not that animals have more imagination than we have given them credit for; on the other hand, it seems to suggest that human beings, like animals, are instinctively deceptive.

Deception is not necessarily an intelligent response. Perhaps Mata Hari was no more intelligent than the moth that spreads its wings to display a pair of terrifying eyes; she was merely doing what came naturally.

In his essay on "Religion and Morals," H. L. Mencken suggests that animals may even have morals.

> It may be argued that such acts and attitudes (as seem inspired by morality) in the lower animals are purely instinctive, and that it would be irrational to dignify them by calling them moral. But to that it may be answered that the motives and impulses lying behind many of the moral concepts of human beings seem to be instinctive in exactly the same sense, and almost to the same extent.

It is interesting to think that we are patriotic and industrious for the same reason that ants are.

But I can say I never knew a moral cat.

BOOKS, MUSIC

I Will Never Catch Up

I have always intended to write a book called *Confessions of a Failed Literary Person*.

I don't know who would read it except a few people, like me, who have not read all the books one is supposed to have read.

The other day I received a note from a friend and colleague saying that he had at last finished reading the entire *Story of Civilization*, by Will and Ariel Durant.

What shame I felt.

I started reading the Durants' series back in the 1930s when the first volume, *Our Oriental Heritage*, was published. I read the third volume, *Caesar and Christ*, in pocketbook form on a troop ship headed for Iwo Jima.

But the Durants could write faster than I could read, and after the war I fell behind. They finished *The Age of Napoleon* before Will and Ariel died, but I was still in *The Renaissance*.

I know now that I will never catch up. In the beginning I meant to read everything. I cut out Mortimer Adler's list of "100 Great Books," which no educated person could afford not to read, and set out to read them all. I'd be surprised if I've read twenty of them.

As a boy I read most of Mark Twain. In my youth I

121

122   read feverishly, if without direction. I read the books that
heated my generation. I read most of Hemingway and most
of Fitzgerald. I read every word that Thomas Wolfe published. That was before I needed eyeglasses.

But after one has a job and a wife and children, the
fever wanes; the appetite fails; the thirst no longer tor-
ments.

In early middle age I became aware of certain land-
marks I had missed. At a tea one afternoon in Hancock
Park I met Rosemary Sisson, a British TV writer, who confessed, when I mentioned it, that she had not read *Alice in
Wonderland.*

I could hardly believe it. A British writer not having
read *Alice in Wonderland!* It was like an American writer
not having read *The Adventures of Huckleberry Finn.*

She was so embarrassed by her lapse that I decided to
confess mine. I had never read *The Adventures of Huckleberry Finn.*

She could hardly believe it.

I have since read *Huckleberry Finn* twice.

But I'm a long way from catching up.

I didn't even read *Lady Chatterley's Lover* until I was
past fifty. It hardly seems possible that I could have en-
dured my youth without reading that forbidden fruit. Having read *Lady Chatterley's Lover* was an essential part of the
equipment of any college man, and one of course had read a
copy that had been smuggled in through customs.

Actually, I liked *Lady Chatterley's Lover* better than
Huckleberry Finn, perhaps because I was already middle-
aged.

Another landmark book in the education of any youth
was *Madame Bovary,* to which I also was not exposed until
my later years. I had always heard that Flaubert was a
master stylist, but, alas, I encountered him too late to profit
from his influence.

I set out once to read the Bible, but when I ran into
Numbers I began to skip. To this day there are many chapters of it that have escaped my scrutiny.

Of the great foreign novels, I read *Les Misérables* as a boy and was in love for a long time with the waif Cosette. One of my true accomplishments is that I also read *War and Peace,* having tackled it under favorable circumstance while working on the night desk of the *Honolulu Advertiser* during the blackout in the first year of World War II. There was nothing else to do.

Although I did read *Crime and Punishment,* I failed miserably in several attempts at *The Brothers Karamazov.* I am told it is one of the great novels, but I foundered on it like a bark on a rock.

I keep trying, however, to patch the gaps in my education. Only the other day I ordered a six-volume biography of Thomas Jefferson. He was perhaps the most admirable of Americans. I am reminded of John F. Kennedy's remark, before an assembly of brilliant guests in the White House. "Ladies and gentlemen, there are more brains gathered in this room tonight than at any time since Jefferson dined here alone."

I feel that as an American I ought to know all I can about Thomas Jefferson. No shortcuts. Read the whole set.

So far I am through page 103 of the first volume. Jefferson is still a young member of the House of Burgesses in Williamsburg, Virginia.

So now when people ask me what I'm reading these days, I say, "Well, I'm into Dumas Malone's "Jefferson and His Time."

Most of them not only haven't read it; they haven't even *heard* of it. It puts me one up.

The truth is I keep regressing. I go to bed fully intending to read myself to sleep with Jefferson, but instead I pick up the latest Elmore Leonard or Robert B. Parker mystery novel, and Thomas Jefferson has to wait another day.

One thing I do promise myself. If I ever finish Thomas Jefferson, I'm going to try *The Brothers Karamazov* again.

Alone on a Desert Island

KCRW, the National Public Radio station in Santa Monica, is doing a series called *Desert Island Disks*, in which selected persons are asked what ten records they would like to have if they were cast away alone on a desert island with no hope of imminent rescue.

Nikola Lubitsch called me from the station the other day and asked if I'd mind being one of the castaways, adding that I would also be asked what one book I would want to take with me and what one luxury item.

"The Bible and the complete works of Shakespeare are out," she said.

Somehow I misunderstood her about the records, thinking she'd said only one record was to be allowed, too, but when she and John McNally arrived at my house one morning a few days later to borrow the records I'd selected, they said it was ten records, not one.

Thinking I could take only one, I had decided on one with a couple of Bach fugues on it, not because I knew them well but because I didn't. I had always felt, when listening to Bach, that a lot was happening that I didn't understand, wasn't even consciously hearing, and that the more I heard the more it might mean. I wouldn't be likely to get tired of it no matter how many years I was stranded. I might even learn to hum along.

"One thing bothers me," I told them. "How are you going to play your records on a desert island? You'd have to have a phonograph, too, and a wall plug."

McNally waved a hand. "We don't worry about that," he said.

I had to think of nine more records. That gave me room to indulge the whole spectrum of my taste. Favorites came to mind. Mozart, of course. *"Eine kleine Nachtmusik."* That would be jolly for the cocktail hour. Beethoven's First. Not somber, not profound. Light as a dancing bear. Good way to start the day. Either *The Pirates of Penzance* or *H.M.S. Pinafore.* Hard choice, there.

"What'll I Do?" if it was Bernadette Peters. Jo Stafford's "I'll Be Seeing You." That was my song of World War II, and it was not a lovely war, but oh, what a lovely song.

I'd want one opera. *La Bohème.* I die and am reborn every time I hear "Musetta's Waltz."

"Penthouse Serenade." "I Found a Million Dollar Baby (in a Five and Ten Cent Store)." Two songs of the Depression. Take your choice.

"Mai Poina," sung by Emma, the Hawaiian thrush. All sorts of trashy hapa-haole music twangs my chords of nostalgia for our two years in the islands, but "Mai Poina" chokes me up, which not even "Praise the Lord and Pass the Ammunition" does anymore.

Leave out the big bands and swing? No way. I'd have to take Glenn Miller's "String of Pearls."

And what to play when I was in the mood for madder music, stronger wine? Offenbach, of course. "Gaieté-Parisienne." At least I could *imagine* the gaiety of the Moulin Rouge and the abandon of the cancan.

And some silver evening, when the surf was murmuring to me and the trade winds were humming their serenade, I'd want to hear Ramón Navarro singing "The Pagan Love Song": "Come with me where moonbeams / Light Tahitian skies. . . ."

If it hadn't been for hearing Navarro sing that song in the Whittier Theater in one of the early talkies, I'd probably never have gone to sea and been shipwrecked in the first place.

You may be shocked at the ones I've left out. But remember—you have only ten, and every time you add one, you lose one. I had to leave out "All Alone by the Telephone," for example, and "Me and My Shadow" and "The Marine Hymn."

As for the book, I wouldn't have chosen the Bible or the complete works of Shakespeare, anyway, even if the rules allowed it. I would certainly like to have them, but if it came down to a single volume, my choice would be the *Merriam-Webster's 3rd International Unabridged Dictionary.*

126   I would prefer the *Oxford English Dictionary*, but even the compact edition comes in two volumes, so I suppose it's not allowed.

While many purists disdain the *3rd International* as "permissive," every word I could ever want to know is in it, and every word is the symbol of an idea that it took the human species millions of years to arrive at. On a Monday, for example, I might run across *solipsism*, the notion that nothing exists or can be proven to exist but the self. Who would be more favorably situated to entertain such a notion than a castaway, alone on a desert island?

It would be something to think about all day, until Tuesday, when I could get up with the sun, play the First Symphony, and look up *serendipity* and think about that.

As for the luxury item, I'd naturally take a magnifying glass so I could read my dictionary.

McNally borrowed all the records I had picked out and will play excerpts from them when I'm on the show. He's hoping to find Bernadette Peters's "What'll I Do?" which I don't have. I know I love it because I heard her sing it on the Academy Awards show, and she sang it the way it ought to be sung.

By the way, if I can't take a magnifying glass, I'm going to ask for a shipload of champagne.

WATCH YOUR LANGUAGE

Where Mountain Cats Still Prowl

By choice, whether wise or not, I rarely employ newly popular words and phrases, such as the currently ubiquitous *burnout* and *state of the art.*

Vogue words tend to be short-lived, and before I resign myself to them, they are often dead of overuse. Burned out.

Thus, I have tried to avoid such vogue words as *viable, input, impact, structured, relevant, meaningful, arguably,* and *skewed.* Too often they give the impression that their users are saying something insightful when they aren't saying anything at all. *(Insightful* ought to be watched, too, by the way.)

I may have slipped and used one or two of them now and then, but only when they seemed exactly right or when I was trying to fake profundity. I am sure, though, that I have never used the current runaway vogue word *total,* or *totally,* except in the sense of the whole amount, or sum.

Excluding the ever-popular obscenities, *total* is the most common adjective and *totally* the most common adverb in American speech today—especially on talk shows, among the rock generation, and in the entertainment world.

It has replaced almost every other descriptive word. One is totally involved emotionally. One's commitment to

127

128   another, or to one's art, is total. One is totally in love. One enjoyed a movie totally.

It is the dream word of the inarticulate. One needn't even think up a sentence to put it in. It stands alone.

"What sort of emotional response do you think *E.T.* inspires in the average moviegoer?"

"Total."

"Did you find it engrossing?"

"Totally."

I have no illusions that my pointing this out will inhibit the meaningless use of *totally* in the slightest. I have already deplored it several times in my columns, only to be totally ignored.

I am inclined myself to totally ignore *burnout* and *state of the art,* but in recent weeks several readers have written to ask where they came from and what they mean, since they have suddenly become fashionable.

Burnout obviously is an aerospace spin-off, meaning, according to Webster's, "the point at which missile fuel is completely burned up and the missile enters its free flight phase," and, also, "damage caused by overheating."

Inevitably, this term has been adapted by human beings to describe their own sense of having exhausted their fuel and been damaged by psychological overheating.

Burnout was made-to-order for psychologists and therapists, who now apply it to their patients in a quasi-scientific way. A publicity release from Indeco, P. O. Box 3252, Orange, announces publication of *I Quit! A Guide to Burn Out Prevention,* by Gayle Levine, M.S., who defines burn out (her spelling) as "the feeling of being used up, having nothing left to give and simply not caring anymore." Happily, however, she adds that "very few cases of burn out are terminal."

The next step in its use, of course, was downward. We are now burned out when we have had a hard day at the office and simply want to pull out of the fast lane, take our shoes off, and have a spritzer. My wife comes home burned out almost every day.

As for *state of the art*, I don't know who started it, but I wish he or she hadn't. One sees it almost every day now, applied to anything from shoes to the ballet. It means, I infer from the context, a performance or piece of work that represents that particular form at its present peak. I'm not sure about that, though. No one ever defines the phrase; they just use it.

Meanwhile, despite Ed Newman and other riders of the Gobbledygook Patrol, our bureaucrats continue to dumbfound us with their cryptic syntax.

Jack Wainschel, an Arcadia physician and gobbledygook watcher, sends a notice that was slipped in with utility bills in the San Francisco area:

> One item of expense included in the rate increase recently granted to PG&E by the Public Utilities Commission, amounting to $177.4 million, was attributable to President Reagan's Economic Recovery Tax Act of 1981, which requires the Public Utilities Commission to charge rate payers for the expense of taxes which are not now being paid to the Federal Government and which may never be paid. This expense may increase in the future.

"My brother-in-law, a nuclear physicist," Wainschel says, "was unable to unscramble it. I was unable to help him. Perhaps you can untangle the convoluted syntax. Thank you for your help."

I'm sorry that I can't help. I haven't the slightest idea what the Public Utilities Commission is trying to say. Whatever it is, though, I suspect it isn't viable. Totally.

To clear the air, I would like to quote a passage sent me recently by Bill Sandlo, of Creative Services, from Agnes de Mille's autobiography, *Dance to the Piper:*

> It's no accident that California produced our greatest dancers, Duncan and Graham, and fostered the work of St. Denis, Doris Humphrey, Maracci and

LaLaLand

130   Collins. The Eastern states sit in their folded scenery, but in California the earth and sky clash, and space is dynamic. When people speak of Hollywood, I am not minded of the goings-on in the hot studios, nor the pleasant social life of cheap oranges and easy swims, but of the untouched country beyond the town, pagan, pantheistic, where mountain cats still prowl, the little deer start and tremble at human approach, coyotes scream and the beneficent rain comes down into the eucalyptus groves.

I prescribe those words for burnout.

I'm Paranoid, You're Paranoid

Among the many words that have been made meaningless by overuse and misuse in these days of instant noncommunication is *paranoia*, which once meant a mental disorder characterized by irrational suspicion or delusions of persecution.

Paranoia, or more exactly the adjective *paranoid*, was debased in the 1960s by young people who used it in disparagement of everyone who was anxious about anything, which meant almost all of us. That our anxiety was quite reasonable was considered irrelevant, *irrelevant* being another word that they rendered void by indiscriminate use.

Nowadays, anyone who has the slightest fear about anything is labeled paranoid. If I am afraid that when I leave my new car in a supermarket parking lot somebody will open his door and ding it, I am paranoid. This happened to me just the other night.

I am reminded of a managing editor I once worked for years ago, on a now-defunct newspaper, who once required me to write that a certain child molester (which he pronounced mole-ster) was a werewolf. "But boss," I protested, "what are we going to call it if they ever catch a *real* were-wolf?"

We are pretty much in that position now with real para-noids.

All of us, of course, are a little bit crazy, and all are given to one obsessive fear or another. It is common to call these fears phobias, from *phobos,* the Greek word for "fear," and then to give them a Greek or Latin prefix that only pedants and psychologists understand.

Thus, the very common fear of closed places is called claustrophobia—*claustra* coming from the Latin *claustrum,* or *cloister,* "a closed-in place."

Others most of us know or have heard are *acrophobia,* "fear of high places"; *nyctophobia,* "fear of the dark"; *ochlophobia,* "fear of crowds"; *xenophobia,* "fear of strangers," and *zoophobia,* "fear of animals."

Like paranoia, a phobia is not simply a sensible fear but an "anxiety hysteria," a psychoneurosis or mild psychiatric disorder, perhaps deriving from some forgotten childhood experience. A person who once almost fell from a window, for example, may become acrophobic.

No field of medicine seems to have given word coiners so much fun. They simply discover or invent a specific kind of fear, look up an appropriate Greek or Latin word to de-scribe it, add *phobia,* and presto, they have contributed an impressive word to the dictionary, if not the living language.

Most of us will never learn any but the most common phobia words, but it is interesting to hear some of the more obscure ones because they are clues to the plethora of fears that our mortal flesh is heir to.

The editors of Merriam-Webster, in a recent "news-letter," list some of the less commonly known phobias that can be found in their unabridged dictionary, the *Third International,* among them *satanophobia*—"an abnormal fear of Satan." (It makes me wonder what they call a normal fear of Satan.)

Erythrophobia, the editors note, is "a morbid fear of the color red." It is this phobia that is thought to enrage the

132   bull in the arena, though I have always doubted it. Don't bulls see everything in shades of gray?

We may laugh at *triskaidekaphobia*, "fear of the number 13," but some of our most modern hotels and skyscrapers still skip from the twelfth to the fourteenth floor, for fear of losing triskaidekaphobic patrons.

Frederick C. Mish, Merriam-Webster's editorial director and a man wonderfully named to run a dictionary, thinks that some of the phobias are not really common in medical practice but were coined for the sheer gamesmanship of it. *Cherophobia*, for example, is "the fear of happiness." I don't know. I've seen lots of movies in which the heroine was said to be afraid of happiness. Bette Davis was often cherophobic.

Then there is *taphephobia*, "the fear of being buried alive." Just to go about fearing that somebody is going to bury you alive may be a phobia, or paranoid; but it seems to me that if there is any chance somebody really is going to bury you alive it is certainly not irrational to worry about it.

Brontophobia is "the abnormal fear of thunder." How scared of thunder do you have to be to have brontophobia? We had it bad in that recent storm. I thought one thunderclap was going to collapse our house. My adrenaline spurted, and I think my blood froze. Is that abnormal?

Ideophobia is "fear of ideas or of reason." That's certainly common enough. I know people who are ideophobic about my ideas, and there's nothing irrational about them. My ideas, I mean.

One of my favorites is *symbolophobia*, "fear that one's acts or speech may contain symbolic meanings." Most everyone I know has this. I hope I won't be thought sexist for saying it appears to be more common in women. They are always looking at men in alarm and saying, "I didn't mean anything by that. Don't get any ideas." In the movies, anyway.

I am also bemused by *symmetrophobia*, "an aversion to symmetry." I think I have the opposite, which I suppose would be asymmetrophobia. I don't like things to be asymmetrical, like women's dresses that fall off one shoulder but not the other. I wonder if I've coined a new one?

If *asymmetrophobia* has already been coined, maybe I can be the first with *hiroshiphobia*—"the fear that we will all be incinerated in a nuclear holocaust."

Maybe it isn't the first phobia word coined for a fear of nuclear war, but I'll bet it's the first with a Japanese prefix.

I hope Dr. Mish can work it into his next edition.

THE SOUND OF MUSIC

Good-bye, "Cheek to Cheek"

Speaking of deprovements—so-called improvements that actually make things worse—high on my list is amplification of sound.

It has its purposes. In its most minute application, it helps the hearing impaired to hear. In great open spaces it can bring a speaker's voice to the multitudes—assuming they really want to hear what is being said.

I remember reading that Abraham Lincoln's famous Gettysburg Address, which he delivered on that battlefield, was heard only by a few hundred persons who were close to the speaker's stand.

I have always imagined the crowd straining to hear the president, or not even trying, having just been harangued for two hours by the orator Edward Everett while their children and dogs ran about respectively shrieking and barking.

Mr. Lincoln had reason to believe it when he said, "The world will little note nor long remember what we say here. . . ."

The applause was light. Few in the crowd realized that the president had just delivered one of history's great speeches. Some newspapers even dismissed it as trivial. But

135

136   the words survived the circumstances, and today the speech is a national treasure.

But the speeches of most politicians might just as well drift across the fields unheard, to mingle in space-time with all the banal public utterances of history.

Amplification also raises the sound level of radio signals so that we can sit comfortably in our living rooms and watch a movie or MTV, hear the president talk, or listen to a golden oldie. It also makes telephone conversation possible.

Beyond those few uses, amplification not only destroys the purity of sound; it damages the ear so that in time it is incapable of making fine distinctions.

I realize that amplification is an intrinsic part of hard-rock music; loudness is essentially the message; it is a music that assaults the flesh as well as the sensibilities; for it to be effective, the listener's bones must resonate. Conversation must be obliterated.

Style is style. A whole generation of rock fans has grown into middle age, and new ones keep coming on. We who have lived on the fringe of rock music all these years are not likely to see it go away. "Cheek to Cheek" is not coming back.

What I am complaining about is not rock music but the extreme amplification of traditional music.

Recently my wife and I attended a banquet in the International Ballroom of the Beverly Hilton. There must have been a thousand people there. Surprisingly, since there were many young people in the crowd, the orchestra played music of the 1930s, 1940s, and 1950s for dancing. "Begin the Beguine." "Bewitched, Bothered and Bewildered." "In the Mood."

The dance floor was a patch of hardwood in front of the bandstand. If the orchestra had played without amplification, the dancers would have heard it quite well. But the orchestra played with such high-level amplification that every drumbeat, every bleat of the clarinets, every rumble of the bass viols, was blasted to the walls, galvanizing flesh,

vibrating eardrums, deadening conversation. At our tables
we were obliged to shout to one another just to exchange
the most basic pleasantries.

Why? If the music had not been amplified, it would still
have reached the outermost tables, arriving sweet and light
and making a pleasant background to conversation.

Years ago, before amplification, I remember going with
my parents to a restaurant downtown where a string trio
played Viennese waltzes. They wore dark blue serge suits
and looked like Sigmund Freud. Their music was faint, distant, romantic.

Later, in my teens, I went once or twice to the Palomar
or the Rainbow Gardens to hear Benny Goodman. There
was no amplification in the contemporary sense. But the
music was loud enough all over the ballroom, and if we
wanted to get closer, to feel it thump, to feel an intimacy
with Goodman, we danced closer to the bandstand and just
stood there in a pack, swaying back and forth like sea plants
at the bottom of the ocean.

I remember reading, years ago, that the Viennese
scholar Ludwig von Kochel first heard Mozart's music while
strolling through a park in Vienna one Sunday afternoon. It
was *"Eine kleine Nachtmusik,"* and Kochel realized at once
that his life had been changed. Soon after that he began his
exhaustive cataloging of Mozart's music.

I wonder whether Kochel would have been so stricken
had "Eine kleine Nachtmusik" been pumped through the
park by powerful amplifiers. There is a sweetness, a deli-
cacy, a lilting quality about that serenade that can not survive a massive amplification.

Years ago I went to the Pleasure Faire out in the West
Valley. Here and there a musical group would be playing
Elizabethan airs without amplification. Amplification was
not allowed. It was regarded as anachronistic. The music
floated over the hills and vales like a leaf on the wind, sweet,
gentle, poignant, seductive. That's the way all music must
have sounded in Elizabethan times.

I don't object to rock music's lyrics, its themes, or its

138 beat. But I can't take its loudness, which is why it's loud. It's meant to demoralize us.

Loudness, like smog and toxic waste, is a destructive product of our technology.

Farewell to "The Sheik of Araby"

I was driving home the other day over the Santa Ana Freeway in a sunset. From some points on the freeway system a sunset can be gorgeous; from the Santa Ana, it usually isn't. It's just something that gets in your eyes.

I was going north of west, though, so the sun was off to my left and was giving the sky a red-gold cast without blinding me. The traffic wasn't bad, and I found myself floating in the sunset, loosened from reality. Vaguely, I was back in another time and place. Not an exact time and place but somewhere else.

Dawn and sunset are the best times of day to slip away from the present. Dawn is open to the future—fresh, new, boundless, exciting, unknown. A sunset contains the past— it stirs remembrance, reflection; it puts the present in perspective.

I had turned the radio to KPRZ, which has specialized for the past few years in the music of my life. They call it "The Music of *Your* Life," but of course every listener who is more than forty years old thinks of the "your" as meaning himself. (Make that fifty years old—even the *Beatles* are forty!)

Jo Stafford had just sung "Long Ago and Far Away." They must have played that for me, knowing I was heading home through the sunset, alone. "Long Ago and Far Away" is one of my faded treasures, locked away in a chest of mementos like a wartime letter; and Jo Stafford has the key.

In the reverie set off by that mystic rendition, I was not

really listening to the disk jockey's patter. He had been talking about a story in the paper—one I'd evidently missed —and phone calls to the studio, and now he was saying yes, folks, he was sorry to say so, but it was true. He might as well come out with it so they'd know and quit calling.

Come out with what? I had tuned in KPRZ because I didn't want any news for a while. I wanted the music of my life. But since he was carrying on about it so, my curiosity was up. So they'd know about what?

"It's true," he said. "Beginning January first, KPRZ is changing its format to rock 'n' roll. No more music of your life. I'll be out on the street—with the other guys."

The sunset was ruined. Just a mean red glare. The music of my life had just been stopped. It was the final triumph of rock 'n' roll.

The world was flat, after all, and my generation was being shoved off the end into the abyss. They were even turning off our radio, as if we were little kids being sent to bed early.

I drove on, unaware of what it was that Artie Shaw was playing. Whatever it was, it was the Death March of KPRZ. Long live rock 'n' roll.

The deejay—I think he was Tom Clay—had said he'd be "out in the street," but he'd be going to some other station. I supposed there were other ramparts still holding out against the barbarians of rock (and the news, sports, talk, religion, and the Dow Jones report), which seemed to have captured the airwaves. But KPRZ was a staggering loss. It was like the loss of France in World War II, when it seemed as if civilization itself were going down.

I don't hate rock if it isn't too loud, especially now that we can see it on video. Some of it is great music, and some of it is poetry, and some of it is pretentious, and some of it is outrageous. I even like some of the outrageous stuff. I love Cyndi Lauper. The one that bops. Believe it or not, she's my type. That is, you know, when I'm not in my Deborah Kerr mood.

I met the Beatles personally on their first American

140   tour, before most of today's rock generation were old enough to say, "She bops." So a large part of my career has coincided with the rise of rock. But the music of my life is the music of the big bands, of jazz, of the silly songs of the Depression and the sentimental ballads of the war; of Louis Armstrong and Glenn Miller and the Dorseys and Bing and Bob and Benny Goodman and all those thrushes who traveled with the bands, like Jo Stafford and Helen O'Connell and Doris Day and Peggy and Ella; and if you want to go a long way back, Rudy Vallee.

I wondered if Gary Owens and Dick Whittinghill and the other KPRZ people who had made KPRZ such fun, and made it human, were going to be out on the street, too; or would they stay and start spinning rock 'n' roll? They could do it, of course. They were pros. But I hoped they wouldn't. I hoped they'd go in a body to some other station and demand that they take up the banner, that they play the music of my life.

KPRZ did public service, too, you know, besides just playing old music to gratify my generation. Just the other night I tuned in when they were observing National Education Week, and they played "Teacher's Pet," "An Apple for the Teacher," and "Teach Me Tonight." Made you think.

And now they tell me they're going to chuck that kind of responsible programming for—well, for what?

I wonder if I'll ever hear Harry James play "The Sheik of Araby" again.

José, Can You See?

With Atty. Gen. Ed Meese's puritanical campaign against pornography and the Supreme Court's intrusion into bedrooms, the heat may be temporarily diverted from rock music for its alleged obscenity and satanism. We're too busy denouncing skin magazines and criminalizing gays to pay much attention to the dirty words that are said to be corrupting our young by way of records, tape, TV, and concerts.

The attorney general's commission on pornography and the court's decision on sodomy have opened up two new fields of prosecution for the rampaging moralists. They don't need rock. However, the Parents Music Resource Center (PMRC), which prodded Congress into hearings on obscene rock lyrics, has not abandoned its crusade.

I have always doubted that the lyrics of rock music could corrupt the young because I don't believe anybody ever really hears them. This belief is rooted in having listened to rock music for more than twenty years now (how can you escape it?) and except for a couple of the old Beatle songs, when they were in their mellow Sergeant Pepper period, never having been able to understand the words.

Most rock music sounds to me like an airplane crash, with the words lost in the general din. Those words that do get heard are usually so banal and repetitious that if you try to listen to them they will hypnotize you, which may be the idea. They are not exactly sung but snarled, or delivered in a primal scream, with amplification so great that what are supposed to be love songs, perhaps, sound more like the agonies of hell or the snorts of the slaughterhouse.

So I am gratified by a recent story in the paper about a survey of 266 junior high and high school students at California State Fullerton. In a forty-page questionnaire, the kids were asked to name their three favorite songs and describe what they were about.

As *Newsweek* commented on the story, the kids came to the same conclusion Mick Jagger had: "It's only rock 'n' roll."

Of the 622 songs named, only 7 percent were thought to be about sex, violence, drugs, or satanism; 26 percent were thought to be about love. They had no idea what 37 percent of them were about. They just liked the beat or the melody.

In other words, about 63 percent of the songs rock fans like best are either about love or nothing identifiable. I think a survey of us survivors of the big-band era would

142 turn up about the same percentage; 63 percent of the songs we liked were either about love or nothing.

Said Lorraine Prinsky, one of the two professors who conducted the test:

> One of the conclusions we came to is that parents are hearing more sophisticated themes in songs than their children are capable of understanding. As for brainwashing kids, or corrupting them, music is a minor factor, if any. . . . Specific lyrics seem to be of little consequence to most kids.

But Jennifer Norwood, administrative assistant of the PMRC, said, on hearing of the study, "It's ridiculous to say that music does not have an effect on human behavior."

Well, my favorite rock star is Cyndi Lauper, and what made her famous was a song whose only words, as far as I can remember, were "She bop." I don't know whether Ms. Lauper's performance would have corrupted me had I been a teenager, but if so, it wouldn't have been the words. It was her style.

The words of songs in any era are treacherous when we try to learn them just from hearing them sung. How children love to sing that old Christian hymn "Gladly the cross-eyed bear!"

William Safire, the *New York Times* word watcher, notes the ways in which children mangle "The Star Spangled Banner."

They sing "José, can you see by the Donzerly light," "o'er the ramrods we washed," and "grapefruit through the night that our flag was still there"!

American soldiers similarly mangled songs they heard overseas. In Japan the popular Japanese song "Shi-i-na-na Yaru" was translated by Americans into "She Ain't Got No Yo-Yo." And what the doughboys did to "Mademoiselle d'Armentières" is unprintable, even today.

I have a letter from Jack K. Walker of Santa Monica who recalls a song written by Joe Maphis, a guitarist who had played on several of Walker's recording sessions. Walker had always thought the song was "Dem Light Sticks Smoke," and it wasn't until he was reading Maphis's obituary that he found out it was "Dim Lights, Thick Smoke."

When he was teaching guitar at a music school to help support his songwriting habit, a student asked Walker if he would teach her the song 'One Ton of Metal." Walker said he didn't know it. The girl hummed a few bars, and Walker recognized it as a recent hit, "Guantanamera."

The student had thought the words were "One ton of metal, why he loads one ton of metal."

Later, Walker told the story to a sophisticated young student who didn't seem to think it was very funny. After an awkward silence, she said, "Actually, I thought it went 'Once on a meadow, while we were once on a meadow.' "

Remember Melina Mercouri, the happy hooker in *Never on Sunday?* She liked to go to the ancient theater in Athens to watch the great Greek tragedies, in ancient Greek. She didn't understand a word of ancient Greek; and when the plays ended, she would jump up cheerfully and say:

"And then everybody went to the seashore!"

That's the way I feel about rock lyrics.

You and Me and Leslie Groovin'

I have been informed by several young readers that the words to "She Bop" are indeed X-rated.

Writes Sidney Hotchkiss of El Toro:

As a college student who enjoys many kinds of music I too believe that most people don't know what they are listening to. However, it is funny that you chose the Cyndi Lauper song "She Bop" to show how one can enjoy a song with meaningless lyrics.

144

What is ironic is that that song is about female masturbation.

This supports your claim that most people are unaware of what they listen to, but it also shows that many mainstream pop songs are not totally innocent.

I didn't say the songs were innocent. I said nobody could understand the words so it didn't matter. *I'm* the one who's innocent.

Gabe Grigolla of Glendora writes:

Whenever I find myself defending rock music to a music lover of another generation I encourage them to listen and try to understand the beauty and wonderful freedom in today's music.

Had you done so with your favorite Cyndi Lauper song, you might have realized that the subject of that particular piece is masturbation.

That interpretation of "She Bop" is also verified by Tom Broderick of Pasadena:

"Cyndi Lauper's 'She Bop' is a classic case of clever innuendo and double entendre. What it's really about is female masturbation! Don't feel bad. I never figured it out till somebody told *me.*"

And by Jay Shaffer of San Francisco:

" 'She Bop' is an ode to onanism."

Shaffer points out that the lyrics of the swing era weren't entirely innocent, either:

I can't see Madonna's "Papa Don't Preach," which is about a teenager who doesn't want to give up the baby with which she is "illegitimately" pregnant, as anything but the result of the confrontation documented in "I Really Must Go (But Baby It's Cold Outside.")

I hear "Baby It's Cold Outside" every now and then among the unforgettables on KMPC, and it is indeed a naughty song.

We also had such shockers as "I Wanna Be Bad" and "Teach Me Tonight."

Shaffer adds:

> I guess my point is that there is no point. Those with dirty minds who are dedicated to looking for evil in every note will find it. Those who like to sing along will decide for themselves whether or not they like the lyrics. Those other 67% or so will go on jogging with the rhythm or pounding on the dashboard with the drums or playing air guitar on the riffs—and will continue to care less until someone tells them they're damned for having a good time. . . .

Several readers have written to sympathize with musician Jack K. Walker's report that a guitar student of his thought the hit song "Guantanamera" actually went "One ton of metal, why he loads one ton of metal" and another student thought it was "Once on a meadow, while we were once on a meadow. . . ."

Ormly Gumfudgin, historian of the World Chili Society, writes that the championship One Ton Tomato Chili Team got its name from a mistaken hearing of that song.

John D. Pickett, a San Diego attorney, writes that when he was growing up in Minnesota, he thought the words to "Guantanamera" were "Once on a meadow, tequila, once on a meadow."

Deborah Blankenberg of Rowland Heights recalls that her favorite example of misunderstood lyrics was a song of the mid-1960s—"Groovin."

> For about 15 years I never admitted my puzzlement at the lyrics, "Life will be ecstasy / You and me and Leslie / Groovin'." Then I heard a San Francisco comedian talking about rock lyrics. He sang those lines

146   and then asked, "Did you ever wonder who Leslie was?" Only then did I learn that "and Leslie" was actually "endlessly."

Alexia St. Germaine of San Diego recalls another hit of the early swing era that went "Mairsey dotes 'n' dosey dotes and little lambsey divey, a kiddley divey too, wooden you?," a classic example of the Guylum Bardo effect, which, when translated, comes out "Mares eat oats and does eat oats, and little lambs eat ivy, a kid'll eat ivy too, wouldn't you?"

We'd probably have been just as well off singing "She Bop."

She adds: "I was nearly 16 when I found out the real words, a fact that contributed immeasurably to a then embryonic but inexorably growing sense of inferiority."

(How can anyone with a name like Alexia St. Germaine feel inferior?)

Paul Epps of La Mirada finds sophistication in Bob Dylan's "You're Gonna Make Me Lonesome When You Go," in which he compares his relationship with those in the poems of Verlaine and Rimbaud.

"What interests me about this stanza is that of all the people who claim rock lyrics are unsophisticated, not one in 100 would understand the Verlaine and Rimbaud reference. ('Well, I know who Rambo is, but Verlaine . . . ?')"

Let us end on a spiritual note by quoting that popular prayer: "Our Father, who art in Heaven, Howard be thy name. . . ."

HOW TO LIVE LONG

Is Crete the Answer?

As a cardiac patient, I always read those articles in magazines and newspapers that report the latest findings on how to have a healthy arterial system and live longer.

It isn't easy to keep up. One month, cholesterol is in; the next it's out. One month, exercise is good for you; the next it will kill you. The only prohibited vices the medical profession seems consistent about are smoking and eating salt. No problem. I quit smoking twenty-five years ago, and I never use a salt shaker. (I get my salt from bacon.)

But there are some things I won't give up just to live a few years longer. I suppose that if I were confronted with an either/or—either give up *huevos rancheros* or die in one year—I would give up *huevos rancheros*.

I believe the purpose of life is to keep on living and see what happens next. But there are some sacrifices that I would not make merely to live longer.

For example, we're always reading that the Japanese do not die of heart attacks because they live on fish and rice, both of which are low in cholesterol.

I like fish if it's fresh and well prepared, but I'm not crazy about rice in any form. If I were assured that I could live to ninety if I were to eat nothing but fish and rice, I think I'd decline.

Now I have received a note from Dr. Henry Blackburn, director of the Division of Epidemiology, University of

147

148   Minnesota, enclosing a recent paper of his on "the low-risk coronary male."

According to Dr. Blackburn, the man most unlikely to have a heart attack is a Greek shepherd, farmer, beekeeper or fisherman, or a tender of olives or vines; he lives on the island of Crete.

Dr. Blackburn first recalls a satirical portrait of the "low coronary-risk male" by Gordon Myers of Boston, which begins:

"An effeminate municipal worker or embalmer, completely lacking in physical and mental alertness and without drive, ambition or competitive spirit, who has never attempted to meet a deadline of any kind. . . ."

But Dr. Blackburn says his Greek islander is "the man truly most free of coronary risk of all men on earth."

This happy fellow walks to work daily and "labors in the soft light of his Greek isle, midst the droning of crickets and the bray of distant donkeys, in the peace of his land."

For lunch he has a lemonade and a meal at the local café, then a nap at home before going back to work.

For his main meal he has eggplant, mushrooms, vegetables, and country bread dipped in olive oil. Once a week he has lamb, once a week chicken, twice a week fresh fish. After that, salad, followed by dates, Turkish sweets, nuts and fruits, with a glass of the local wine.

Saturday nights he has a festive dinner with family, then parties with friends and takes part in a passionate midnight dance in the grain fields.

Sunday he goes to church and spends a quiet afternoon with his family in the shade, "cooled by the salubrious sea breeze, gently perfumed by smoke from olive-wood charcoal grills, and fragrances wafted from the fields of herbs and fresh animal dung. . . ."

He does not spend his Sunday tied in knots in front of a TV set watching the Super Bowl.

Dr. Blackburn notes that this man of Crete lives in harmony with nature and the landscape, secure in his niche in the long history of Greek civilization.

"He relishes the natural rhythmic cycles and contrasts of his culture: work and rest, solitude and socialization, seriousness and laughter, routine and revelry.

"In his elder years, he sits in the slanting bronze light of the Greek sun, enveloped in a rich lavender aura from the Aegean sea and sky. . . ."

I suppose I could retire and live in the Greek islands, "sitting in the slanting bronze light of the Greek sun. . . ."

But sooner or later, I suspect, I'd begin to crave some stress. I'd miss my daily paper; I'd miss knowing how the Dodgers and the Angels were doing in September; I'd miss going out to dinner and going to the Music Center; I'd miss those trashy miniseries on TV; I'd miss the National Football League; I'd miss my family.

Of course my wife would be with me. Otherwise, who'd cook my eggplant? But I'm afraid I'd never feel at home. I would have no feeling of my niche in history.

Here, after all, is where I belong, in the wonderful wasteland of Los Angeles, here on the freeways, here in my hot tub, here with my bacon and eggs and Big Macs and *huevos rancheros* and Mexican beer. Here with my books and my TV and my daily avalanche of junk mail. Here in La La Land.

Maybe we'll just go to Crete this year for a visit.

I'd like to try the local wine and dance passionately in the moonlight.

"I'm Keeping My Husband in Pasadena"

A cardiologist's fantasy of the man who lives a long and sensuous life on the island of Crete, free of cardiovascular deterioration, has been shattered.

Evidently Crete is not the salubrious Elysium described by my correspondent, Dr. Blackburn.

150   Antoinette Dungan of Visalia has evidently been to Crete and found it less than idyllic.

"Our senior citizen of Crete," she writes, "must use a quart of insect repellent every day and must sleep under a mosquito net in order to live the blissful life you so eloquently describe.

"Thank goodness for our Tulare County Mosquito Abatement District which indirectly helps me live the peaceful life here in Visalia!"

Writes Joyce Helfand of Tujunga:

I truly believe that you are being deluded if you think for a moment that you could live longer if you retired to live on the Greek island of Crete, especially if you lived the life of a typical man of Crete.

Dr. Blackburn does not know what he's talking about. To take issue with each of his points would give me a heart attack. But let me tell you this: The passionate midnight dance he refers to lasts well into the morning hours of church-going Sunday. Most often it is a dance called "Pentozali," and literally means "five dizzy steps." I have danced it and seen it danced, and I assure you it can make strong men weak and weak men die.

As far as food is concerned, and eggs in particular, no one said it better than the great Nikos Kazantzakis, himself a passionate Cretan. I quote from his work, "Freedom or Death."

"There are three sorts of men: those who eat eggs without the shells, those who eat eggs with the shells and those who gobble them up with the shells and the eggcups as well. The third kind are called Cretans. . . ."

Sofia Adamson, founding trustee of the Pacific Asia Museum, writes to warn me that life in Crete is much more complicated than Dr. Blackburn supposes:

It is no longer just "dancing passionately in the moonlight." We discovered last August at the El Greco Hotel in Rethymnos, Crete, that hundreds of buxom, blonde hausfraus of Germany, Sweden and Britain and other cold-swept reaches of northern Europe come to Crete to soak up the sunshine, topless, on its alluring beaches.

My husband and I had an eyeful. He had open heart surgery in 1979, and I feared for him. Our hotel balcony had a full view of these developments. . . .

Actually, Mrs. Adamson hasn't said anything so far that would prohibit my going to Crete, at least not for medical reasons. I, too, have had heart surgery, but that was two or three years ago, and I think I have now recovered to the point where I could quite safely view the developments she speaks of.

In fact, there might actually be a rehabilitating force in the sight of rows of topless northern European hausfraus displayed voluptuously in the slanting bronze light of the Greek sun.

I might not be able to dance the Pentozali, but a little innocent voyeurism would probably do me good.

Mrs. Adamson continues:

Also, on the south side, facing Libya, the hippies of 10 years ago took to living in caves and creating the nude-bathing beaches, which surely have given quite a few of the Cretans heart attacks. Now, the suddenly-affluent village of Plakia has been filled with curiosity seekers. Two major new hotels are being built to accommodate the curious Greeks.

So, Mr. Smith, there goes Crete and its low coronary-risk males; there's a new version of 'passionate dancing in the Cretan moonlight' complicated by hausfraus and hippies.

I'm keeping my husband in Pasadena.

152   As I noted, I had no intention of leaving home and going to Crete, even if it might mean a longer life. I was not attracted to dancing in the moonlight and eggplant meals with the local wine. I prefer the complexity of life in Los Angeles, where I have the Dodgers and my newspaper and those trashy miniseries on TV.

Among the communications I received about Dr. Blackburn's theory was a telegram from the actor Eddie Albert, evidently a man of healthy appetites. I have mislaid Mr. Albert's message, but as I remember, it read something like this:

"WOW! CRETE! WHEN ARE WE LEAVING?"

I don't know how Mr. Albert will feel about Crete after he reads Mrs. Adamson's letter, but maybe we could both slip over there for a couple of weeks this spring. I could leave my wife in Pasadena.

Of course we'd have to remember to take some insect repellent.

STATE OF THE ART

Please Leave Your Number

Although I have owned a state-of-the-art telephone answering machine for two or three years, no caller has ever heard its voice.

I have taped several answers, trying to get one I liked, but none was satisfactory.

For one thing, I don't like to call someone and get an answering machine, so I assume that no one likes to call me and get an answering machine.

I sometimes think I'd rather just get a no answer than a taped message:

"Hello. This is Fred. I'm not available to answer the phone right now, but please wait until you hear the tone, then leave your name . . ."

Of course, we have hung up long before we get that far.

There is also implicit in that kind of message a promise to return the call, and I get some calls I'd rather not return. But when you have invited the caller to leave his name and number and promised to call him back, you have to. It's plain courtesy.

Of course, Fred's message is routine. It gets the job done. It's the cute ones that knock me off my trolley. Then there are the sexy ones, miniseductions that you know are never going to result in any consummation. If you leave

153

154 your number and they call you back, they are quite matter-of-fact about it, no sexual innuendos at all, and they always ask for your wife.

I am also put off by the feeling that the person I've called is in and is listening to my message but doesn't want to talk to me. He may call me back when he's good and ready or not at all. This puts him in a position of power over me that I don't like.

When my older son's answering machine was on the blink recently, he borrowed mine for a couple of weeks. That's the only service it's seen. It worked perfectly well for him, and he doesn't understand why I don't use it.

One of the problems is that playing back our message gives us a chance to hear how we sound to others, and it isn't always flattering. On tape I don't sound like Orson Welles or Ronald Colman or even like Laurence Olivier. I sound more like Donald Duck or Jack Smith.

Some years ago I had an earlier-model answering machine, and I tried to use it. At that time we were remodeling our house, and our contractor had his own answering machine. He was never in when I called him, so I would leave a message on his machine. Then he would call back when I wasn't in and leave a message on my machine. I got the eerie feeling that our machines were communicating but we weren't, and it wasn't long after that that I gave the machine to one of my sons and sank back into the eighteenth century.

I bought the new one later because I love gadgets and can't resist having the latest thing. But now I have this problem, which, as far as I know, is purely psychological. There is nothing mechanically wrong with the machine. Murphy's Law hasn't had a chance to set in.

Maybe my problem is that I haven't worked out a message that reveals my personality.

I have received a publicity handout from a company named Record a Call, which is celebrating the twenty-fifth anniversary of the answering machine, and it reports that many "creative owners" have managed to give their messages a personality that reflects their own.

Others have fun by taping their messages in imitation of such easily recognized voices as those of Ronald Reagan, Walter Cronkite, Cary Grant, and so on. I imagine women might go for Katharine Hepburn.

This phenomenon got some of the Record a Call people to thinking about famous persons of the past and what kind of messages they might have left if they had had answering machines.

For example:

Sigmund Freud: "At the tone, please tell me your name, tell me your phone number, and tell me how you feel about your mother."

Adam: "I can't come to the phone right now. I'm out buying some spare ribs."

George Washington: "I cannot tell a lie. I am in, but I'm not answering the phone."

Michelangelo: "Sorry I can't come to the phone; right now I'm flat on my back."

Moses: "I'd answer my phone but I keep getting these crank calls from some guy named De Mille. He thinks I'd be perfect for the lead in *The Charlton Heston Story.*

Captain of the Titanic: "I'd like to talk to you, but it's been a long day, and now I want a little something on ice."

Mata Hari: "At the beep, leave a secret."

I've tried thinking of some myself:

Judge Crater: "I'm out, and I don't know where I've gone."

Harold Stassen: "Sorry, I'm out running for president."

Napoleon: "Call me back after Waterloo."

Jimmy Carter: "I think you want Ronald Reagan."

Ronald Reagan: "Nancy and I can't answer the phone right now. They won't let us."

Prince: "If you want to talk to me, you have to ask God."

Michael Jackson: "You probably wanted Prince. You can get him at God's."

Richard Nixon: "At this point in time, I'm out. I want to make that perfectly clear."

Tommy Lasorda: "If this is Steve Howe, forget it."

Mae West: "I thought you'd never call."

Charles Manson: "Hi. I've gone away for a while."

Jack Smith: "Please don't call me when I'm out."

I Built for the Ages

My wife found an item in one of her mail-order catalogs that she thought might interest me.

She said, "It's a light bulb that lasts sixty-thousand hours, so you never have to replace it."

I felt a twinge of anxiety.

"Sixty thousand hours?" I said.

"Yes, it says that's long enough to last twenty years if you only burn them eight hours a day."

"The way we leave lights on," I said evasively, "that would only last us about ten years."

Even so, I was worried. "Let me see it," I said.

The ad read:

You never have to change these bulbs. Standing on a ladder, or balancing on a chair, while trying to re-

place a hard-to-reach light bulb in the dark, is one of
our least favorite chores. So we've replaced all our
ordinary bulbs with these patented Diolight Forever
bulbs, guaranteed for 60,000 hours. That's 20 years,
even at eight hours every day!

I felt like an NFL quarterback whose contract has not
been renewed. I was through. Over the hill.

The truth is, changing light bulbs is the only male chore
left to me around the house. I have always regarded changing light bulbs as a job that requires exquisite physical balance, a respect for electricity, good hands, and a certain
amount of engineering intuition.

I don't say that my wife, or any other woman, doesn't
have these skills; but there is the added element of danger.
As the ad implies, balancing on a chair while trying to
change a light bulb is a risky business.

The chair may slide out from under you. Or you may
lose your balance and fall. With your head turned up toward a ceiling fixture and your arms raised, you may become dizzy.

Now and then I have found my wife trying to change a
bulb by herself. She invariably uses a chair, though I have
told her and told her that one must use a ladder, for safety's
sake.

I always say, "What are you doing?"

She says, "I am changing this light bulb. It's been out
for two weeks."

The implication is that she's not only quite capable of
changing the bulb herself but that I have been negligent of
my duty in not changing it for two weeks.

I always instruct her to get down from the chair and
assure her that I will change the bulb immediately.

There are two reasons for this:

One, I don't want her to fall and break a leg or a hip. I
would be absolutely helpless without her, since the only
thing that would get done around the house would be the
changing of light bulbs. I would have nothing to eat, I

LaLaLand

158   would have no ironed shirts, and I would have no one to put out the trash barrels.

Two, if she changed bulbs, there would be nothing left for me to do.

In my hardier years I did concrete work. I built for the ages. In the beginning I didn't know that one could fill a form with empty beer cans, stones, and other debris, to lighten it and to save concrete.

Consequently, the steps I built from the front porch down to the sidewalk are solid concrete. I mixed it all with a shovel in a wheelbarrow and poured it into forms I had built myself. It will never break, erode, or slide.

I also built a beautiful curving downhill walk from the service porch to the front sidewalk. I swept the fresh concrete with a broom to make it slip-proof and give it an attractive texture.

Since then we have lost our milkman, who was the only reason for the walk. Our back door has been permanently locked for years. But that walk is my masterpiece. If we ever sell the house, it will add $5,000 to the price.

I also built concrete steps from the upper level of our backyard to the lower level, twelve steps with two landings. Solid as the Lincoln Memorial. Each step is bound to the next with steel brackets. My steps will never break up or slide. After the Big One has done us in and archaeologists are sifting through the debris of Mt. Washington a century or two from now, they will find those steps and wonder at the determination, ingenuity, and integrity of twentieth-century man.

But I haven't done concrete since my disk slipped. I have never been much good at plumbing or carpentry, and except for changing light bulbs, I don't fool with electricity at all.

So there isn't a lot I can do to prove that I'm still the man of the house, unless that term has been outmoded by the women's liberation movement.

I am very good at light bulbs.

I say it takes engineering intuition. When you are

unscrewing a ceiling globe, for example, you have to remember that the screws on the far side of the globe must be screwed out *clockwise,* not counterclockwise, as with those on your own side. It takes experience to get that straight.

We keep a large supply of bulbs in the linen closet, and whenever a bulb burns out, I get right on the job. At least in a week or two. You have to get yourself mentally organized to change a light bulb.

So I am not about to send away for any light bulbs that are guaranteed to last 60,000 hours, or 20 years, whichever comes first.

Technology is not going to obsolete me.

"I Love You Ever and Ever"

In these days when it is so easy to "reach out and touch someone" by telephone, the love letter is a thing of the past.

What a loss to mankind in passion and poetry.

Even the least literate of us could write a love letter that would bring tears to the eyes of our sweetheart. Honest feelings made the simplest words poignant.

"Dear Mary: I love you. I miss you. I can't wait to be in your arms again. Love. John."

Today the stricken fellow merely dials a number and, when she answers, says, "Hey. How ya doin'?"

A young woman writes, "I write love letters. . . . But what exactly is the relationship of love letters to the teaching (or learning) of English?"

None. Only the most rudimentary grasp of English is required for the writing of love letters.

The young woman goes on:

Despite the convenience of the telephone (yes, ours is an 11-digit relationship) it is my opinion that it discourages intimacy and intimate communication. There is no paper left over to tie up with ribbon. . . . all that remains is the sensation of a tinny

160   voice, and sweaty plastic making a dent in your ear. . . .

The long-distance telephone is a powerful means of communication. In times of disaster, it can reassure someone of a loved one's safety. It can end, if only momentarily, an aching loneliness.

We have always been fascinated by its magic. Louella Parsons used to assure her readers that she had just talked to Carole Lombard or Clark Gable "on the long-distance telephone" and had thus received the confidences she was about to reveal.

We have all been kept cooling our heels in outer offices while secretaries assured us that the man we wanted to see was "talking long distance," a miraculous phenomenon that was expected to impress and placate us.

With the telephone so handy and direct dialing so easy, does anyone write love letters anymore?

I suppose that people who are separated by long distances and who can not afford to telephone each other often may be reduced to taking out pen and paper and attempting to describe their sentiments in writing.

I doubt, though, that the mails are very often heavy with love letters. If separated lovers can't afford to reach out and touch each other by telephone, they will probably be disconnected, like the telephone of a user who does not pay his bill.

Recently I received a small letter opener from Benjor Products, of Torrance. It was sent to me by Marcia Reed of that company with the explanation that they hoped to market them in card shops. They are meant for opening love letters only.

I imagine that a letter opener intended for love letters only will serve just as well for opening bills and junk mail. However, I have put mine aside for use in the unlikely event that I ever receive another love letter.

Ms. Reed had been doing research on love letters and

found that the form goes back at least as far as Cleopatra,

found that the form goes back at least as far as Cleopatra, who sent engraved tablets of onyx and crystal to Antony.

She found that Henry VIII wrote to the luckless Anne Boleyn that he had been "for more than a year struck by the dart of love."

Try to imagine how the conversation might have gone if Henry had been able to dial Anne: "Hey, Anne. Hank here. How ya doin'?"

And Anne might have said, "If you don't quit calling me, King, I'm going to change my number."

Those two cases show that the dart of love does not always bring lasting happiness. Poor Anne had her head chopped off, and Cleopatra put a deadly asp to her breast.

Ms. Reed considers John Keats's letters to Fanny Brawne the ultimate in emotion distilled:

"My dear girl, I love you ever and ever and without reserve. The more I have known you the more have I lov'd. . . . In the hottest fit I ever had I would have died for you. . . ."

What might John have said if he'd dialed Fanny's eleven-digit number and got her on the line: "Hey, Fannie, how ya' doin'?"

The telephone has also outmoded almost every other written form of communication. I have a treasured letter written by the celebrated early nineteenth-century English wit Sidney Smith. It is simply a social note promising to call on a friend.

If Sidney had been able to telephone, I would not have this letter in a frame today. The sound of his message would be lost in the cosmos.

Even the office romance is no longer sustained by those furtive little notes that used to be pressed into open palms, sometimes by confederates. Today office lovers leave messages on each other's computers. The method is private, and the messages can easily be wiped out.

This may be both ultramodern and oh so convenient, but it doesn't leave you anything to tie up in a ribbon.

BRAVE NEW WORLD

As Long as They Have No Taste Buds We're Safe

Ever since I was a small boy life has been threatened by robots. They were going to take over sooner or later.

In the beginning, I think robots were merely a methaphor for industrialized man and were used as bugaboos by social thinkers.

When I was in high school our drama class did *R.U.R.* (*Rossum's Universal Robots*), Karel Capek's 1923 play about a future in which robots, enslaved to do man's work, revolt against their masters. It was great fun. Everyone dressed in robot costumes made of cardboard and walked about in the awkward gait of robots. Nobody took it seriously.

I realize now that *R.U.R.* was more a protest against the enslavement of man by machines than a warning against an uprising of robots in the future. But now, we're told, robots are here, and they're about to take over many of our human tasks.

According to a recent piece in the paper, robots are not yet as sensitive and versatile as human beings, but they are a "formidable presence in our world," and one can do the work of three to five people. The author of the article comforts us with the assurance that robots can't see very well, have no taste buds, and don't have much common sense.

163

164   But already they are doing many menial jobs for us and in time will free us even from mental labor so we can relax and devote ourselves to pleasure and culture.

Robots may not be able to think, but they can beat us at checkers and at backgammon and probably at Scrabble, though I'm not too sure about that. They would have to know a lot of words like *zygote, yuck,* and *uxoricide.*

In another article, only a day or two later, we were told that we will soon be living in smart houses that can water our lawns, take and reroute our calls, cook our breakfast, and turn on lights when we enter a room and turn them off when we leave it.

Is this to be our brave new world? When do robots cease to make our lives more enjoyable?

Sometimes I think we have already reached the point when we should have said, "Stop, enough!" and arrested the invention of ever more human machines. I'm not absolutely sure I want to live in a completely automated house, with robots around to do all the homely little chores.

I'm sure my wife would like a robot to cook dinner, wash dishes, and vacuum the carpet. If we could count on a robot to cook dinner on time, we wouldn't have to make a mad dash to the Music Center, as we usually do.

It might seem like a good idea to have a robot that fed the dogs; but a dog's devotion to his master comes from his master's role as the provider of food, and who wants a dog that loves his robot more than his master?

Now *washing* the dog is something else. I wouldn't mind having a robot that could wash the dog, take the trash out, and clean the bathtub.

I wouldn't mind a robot that went out to pick up the paper, especially on cold and rainy mornings, but of course, in the automated future we may no longer have newspapers. Our news will simply emanate from the walls, perhaps chosen for us by some judicious government censor.

I'm not sure, though, that I'd care to have a robot idling about the house when it wasn't busy. According to the story, roboticists predict that within twenty years some robots will have emotions and self-awareness. I couldn't stand a robot in the house who was pouting because we didn't pay it enough attention or was hurt because of some imaginary reproach.

An idle robot would get on my nerves and on my conscience. I'd keep thinking, I wonder if it would like to play a game of checkers. But who wants to play checkers with something that beats him every time?

With robots growing so sophisticated that they can almost think, I'm afraid that having one around the house would make me feel self-conscious, as if a brother-in-law were living with us. I'd never feel quite free to say what I wanted to say or do what I wanted to do.

But I'm not worried yet. As long as they have no taste buds we're safe. A robot that can't tell a Napa Valley Chardonnay from a Long Beach Diet Pepsi is no threat to civilization.

You Can Spend the Day in Your Pajamas

A public relations man I know has sent me a notice that Record a Call, which he evidently represents, is sponsoring a Home-based Entrepreneur of the Year Award of $1,000, with telephone answering machines going to two runners-up.

My friend also notes that a recent poll conducted by Yankelovich, Skelly and White, who may also be clients of his, shows that "earning a living at home is the secret dream of fully a third of American workers."

He says, "It is estimated that some 10 million people in the United States now have a full or part-time business at home, and that this number could double within the next decade. It is one of the fastest growing sectors of the American economy."

166   As a person who has the privilege of working at home, I certainly know its comforts and advantages. You can spend the entire day, if you feel like it, in your pajamas, robe, and slippers. The refrigerator is never more than a few steps away, and if you happen to want a bottle of beer at ten o'clock in the morning, who's going to be the wiser?

Your car remains safe in your garage, unexposed to dangerous freeway traffic and costly accidents, burning neither rubber nor gasoline, and you do not have to pay ten dollars a day to park it.

If you like music while you work, you can play anything you want on stereo—from Beethoven to Springsteen—and if you don't like music, you are not assaulted continually by the homogenized ambience of Muzak.

If you have an urge to dig in the garden or take a walk, you can leave your work for a while, knowing that your machine will answer any phone calls. You simply record a message saying you're too busy to answer at the moment and no one knows you're not slaving over the word processor.

You are never bothered by fellow workers who want to gossip or get you to help them with their work or try to get a date to go bowling or borrow money or a cigarette. You never have to worry about the office practical joker. You don't even have to worry about sexual pressure.

You are free, independent, isolated, alone—but intimitely connected by telephone and computer to the company.

Your work will reach its destination sooner than if you had to pull it from a typewriter and take it to the next desk.

In the afternoon, after you've had a leisurely lunch of cheese cannelloni heated in the microwave, a tomato and lettuce salad, and half a bottle of chablis, you can nap for half an hour.

In late morning the postman comes, connecting you by mail with the outside world. He may be the only person you see in a week. You begin to look forward to his visits.

You also begin to look forward to the calls of the buxom

young woman who delivers for the United Parcel Service. She is pretty and fresh and cheerful, and you are tempted to invite her in for lunch, but you know, of course, that such tarrying would be against her rules. Besides, the neighbors might talk.

Sooner or later you begin to feel just a little bit lonely. You decide maybe you'll go down to the Mexican place for lunch and a bottle of Carta Blanca. See some people. Play some mariachi on the jukebox.

You begin to think how much fun it used to be working in the office.

In a big corporate office you spend about two-thirds of your time actually working and one-third socializing and gossiping. There are always some office romances going on, and if you aren't actually involved in one, you can at least surreptitiously watch its development. A romance that ripens in an office cannot be hidden. There is that telltale meeting of eyes, the bumping of hips in the cafeteria line, the lingering conversations, the tête-à-têtes at lunch.

If Alice is having an affair with Timothy, there's no way you can know it if you work at home. People can meet, fall in love, go through an office courtship, and get married, and you won't have any idea that it's happening until some morning the postman brings you a wedding announcement.

You miss out on all the office pools. You don't have anyone to discuss the Raiders' quarterback problem with. You want to tell somebody they should stick with Jim Plunkett. But the postman isn't a football fan. The United Parcel delivery person is always in too much of a hurry to discuss football.

The postman always comes up with some wisecrack about the government. He isn't crazy about the system. But he's always in a hurry to get on, and you can't really discuss anything with him in depth.

Sometimes you get so frustrated you decide to have a couple of beers in the afternoon, and naturally the quality of your work goes down.

You begin to wonder if anybody at the company knows

168   you still work for them. You decide you'd better get dressed and go in. This happens to me at least three times a week. I pick up my mail, flirt with all the women, make a few bets on sports events, and drop into the boss's office to make sure he remembers me. Usually I have a fraternal lunch with some of my colleagues.

Working at home alone isn't exactly the dream life it might seem to be.

No Time for Summertime?

In the Berry's World cartoon the other day our hero is sitting on the floor in front of his TV-VCR, surrounded by tape cassettes, and he's saying to his wife, "I'm afraid the only way we can catch up on all the stuff we've taped is to quit our jobs and stay home."

Anyone who owns a videocassette recorder and knows how to use it (which eliminates a good many) can share that feeling.

Though I have owned a recorder for quite a while, I am not diligent in its use. Either I forget to tape shows that I might want to see later, or I set the machine wrong and it doesn't tape. I think part of my indifference is the feeling, deep down, that I'm never going to find the time or the inclination to play a tape back.

When I bought it, my VCR was state of the art. That means it is so complicated I had to have professional help to find out how to work it. I am still intimidated by the procedure required to tape a show that is going to be on the tube a day or two in the future.

I am most reliable at taping a show while we're watching it; but of course there is no great urge to have a tape of a show that you will already have seen. Someday, maybe, you might like to see it again, but if you start taping for the future, you're soon going to have no room for your tape file, and you're going to have a lot of money invested in tapes you'll never have time to see. Some of them are classics.

Even so, despite my apathy, we already have a large and growing library of tapes we have never seen and probably never will see, unless, as Berry suggests, we quit our jobs and stay home. For instance, we still have—and have yet to play back—the wedding of Prince Charles and Princess Di —All that pomp and ceremony and romance captured on tape for all time—and never seen.

We didn't happen to watch the wedding at the time, but somehow it doesn't seem as real and exciting as it did then. Life goes on. The prince and princess have two children now. Their wedding tape would be like pictures in an old album, with the odor of pressed violets.

We still have our tape of the Olympic Games opening-day ceremony. We were there, in the Coliseum, for that stirring spectacle, and perhaps someday we will find the time, and the mood, to replay it in our living room. But it will always be there, waiting, so there's no hurry. Anyway, the excitement of that glorious day, especially those thrilling moments when the American crowd cheered the Romanians and when Rafer Johnson mounted the stairway to light the torch, can never be recreated. A rerun can only make us feel older.

I used to have a tape of Super Bowl XVIII, in which the Raiders, led by my hero Jim Plunkett, demolished the Washington Redskins, 38–9. But, alas, I taped over that game to record, for posterity, the 1984 campaign debate between Geraldine Ferraro and George Bush. Somehow it seemed important at the time. I wish I had Superbowl XVIII back.

I also have a tape of that old movie *Summertime* in which Katharine Hepburn, as an unmarried woman from Akron, Ohio, goes to Venice on a holiday and falls in love with Rossano Brazzi, a married Venetian merchant. We could play that some Sunday evening, I suppose, but we are always seduced away from such old-fashioned sentiment by

170   some semipornographic miniseries like *Hollywood Wives* or *Sins.*

I also have *Grand Hotel* on tape, which is useful mostly for settling arguments. This is the one in which Garbo says, "I want to be alone." She does not say, as some people believe, "I want to be left alone."

This is also the one in which Garbo has her grand passion for John Barrymore, a passion that Garbo somehow managed to suggest without thrashing about in the nude with Barrymore, on the rug, as she would probably be required to do today.

I doubt, though, that I will ever find time to play *Grand Hotel* again. It will probably just gather dust in my archives. But one thing I won't do is tape over it to record the next debate between vice-presidential candidates. I learned my lesson. Nothing goes out-of-date faster than a political debate.

What my VCR has taught me is that we are creatures of the moment. We are always more drawn toward what's new than toward what's good. Today's sequence of *Miami Vice* has more appeal than Reagan's second Inaugural Address (not that Reagan was that good).

One of the reasons I bought my VCR was that it has the capacity to record eight half-hour or four hour-long programs.

It never occurred to me that at no time in my life will I ever be far enough ahead to watch four hours of recorded television.

Still, there is some magic in old film.

As I was writing this, I couldn't remember what town Katharine Hepburn was from in *Summertime.* Cincinnati, Toledo—something like that. I went into the bedroom and started my *Summertime* tape, meaning to play it far enough to find out.

Played it all the way through.

Everyone Knows
What an Atom Is

According to a story in the paper the other day, so-called experts who met at a three-day National Technological Literacy Conference in Baltimore were worried that most of us in America are "technologically illiterate."

That means we don't understand the very technology that facilitates modern life and which, ironically, also threatens its existence.

They stated, for example, that in a national survey of 2,000 adults more than 80 percent did not understand how telephones work, and 75 percent did not have a clear understanding of what computer software is.

I'm afraid that if that is the kind of question they asked I'd turn out to be a technological illiterate myself.

We are all masters, in a way, of our technology. Its genies are ours to command. Its miracles are at our fingertips. Yet few of us understand how our machines and appliances and playthings work.

I have a nightmare in which I am on the witness stand and am being asked all kinds of simple questions about technology.

Q.   Mr. Smith, I assume you have a telephone.

A.   Oh, yes. Use it all the time.

Q.   Just answer the questions, Mr. Smith. Please tell us, in your own words, how the telephone works.

A.   Well, it has this cord, which connects with the wires outside, on the poles, and those wires connect with central, wherever that is, and central has wires going all over the world, so you can call anywhere in the world you want to.

LaLaLand

Q. I see. And what is the energy that carries your voice over those wires?

A. Electricity.

Q. And what is electricity?

A. I haven't the slightest idea.

Q. Then, in fact, Mr. Smith, you don't know how the telephone works.

A. Not really.

Q. Now it is true, Mr. Smith, is it not, that you own a computer?

A. That's right. I own an IBM PC. However, I don't use it for anything but word processing.

Q. And you use a software program for this word processing?

A. Yes. It's called Easy Writer.

Q. And what is software, Mr. Smith?

A. Well, it's this floppy disk, like a little phonograph record. You put it in the computer and turn it on and your Easy Writer program is ready to work.

Q. How does your computer work? What takes place inside the computer that makes it work?

A. Electricity.

Q. But you don't know what electricity is?

A. No, not for sure.

Q. I see. Mr. Smith, do you know what an atom is?

A. Yes, of course. Everyone knows what an atom is.

Q. Please tell us, in your words, what an atom is.

A. Well, it's the smallest unit of matter. Except that it has these even smaller units whirling around inside it. They're called electrons and protons and neutrons, and I think there are some others they've discovered recently that I can't remember the names of.

Q. Mr. Smith, do you know how these particles inside the atom act?

A. I forget. They spin around. I know there's another one called the neutrino, but they don't know whether it has any mass or not.

Q. They don't know whether it has any mass or not?

A. Yes, that's right. I have this friend at Caltech. I had breakfast with him the other morning. He's a nuclear physics engineer. He builds machines in which they try to catch neutrinos.

Q. They try to *catch* neutrinos?

A. Yes. The whole question is whether neutrinos have any mass or not. If they have mass, it changes everything.

Q. What do you mean changes everything.

A. Well, you know the Big Bang theory? That the universe started something like fifteen billion years ago with a big explosion? And that all the stars and planets are hurtling outward through space from the point of this Big Bang?

Q. Go on.

A. Now if the neutrinos don't have any mass, that means that things will go on exploding outward through infinity. So that means the universe will expand forever. But if the neutrino has mass, that means it's as if everything were attached to a rubber band that will stretch only so far, and when it stretches as far as it can, it will

start to retract, and then everything in the universe will start coming back to where it started from.

Q. I see. And what exactly are these neutrinos that may or may not have mass?

A. I haven't the slightest idea. Nobody has ever seen one.

Q. Perhaps you can tell us why, if the neutrino should turn out to have mass, the universe will come back together, so to speak.

A. That's because there are so many neutrinos that if they turned out to have mass, their gravity would sooner or later counteract the force of the original explosion and bring everything back.

Q. Mr. Smith, do you have any idea how large the universe is?

A. No. Carl Sagan says there are more stars than there are grains of sand on all the beaches of the world. I can't conceive of that many stars.

Q. And yet you say that the neutrino, which no one can see, can make all those stars snap back.

A. That's what my friend said at breakfast. I might have got it wrong. I had a glass of champagne.

Q. Would you say, Mr. Smith, that you are technologically illiterate?

A. That's right. No doubt about it.

Q. You may step down.

WORD PROCESSING

The Writer's Secret

As one of thousands of writers who have already converted to the word-processing home computer, I do not miss that preliminary product of a writer's labor—the original manuscript.

When a writer composes on a computer, his mistakes are instantly erased, without a trace, by his corrections, and there is no tortured original manuscript to betray the anguished trial and error behind the finished work.

Writing on a computer screen is like writing in water. The literary manuscript will become a historical curiosity, like the goose-quill pen.

I hadn't thought much about this side effect of the computer revolution until I read a column on the subject by a Professor Toro in the *Monterey Peninsula Herald.*

"One wonders," he says, "what will become of the craft of literary historians. . . . To the writer whose study is the works of other writers, there are few thrills comparable to holding an original manuscript by a fine novelist or poet in his hands, the very words and paper that the great man himself sweated over . . ." (Dr. Toro notes that he means women authors as well as men and uses "the generic masculine" to include both.)

"Something magic is involved in the craft of writing,"

176 he continues, "and to see the rough draft of a story or poem
is to re-experience the creative process. The literary historian revels in detailing the words stricken out in favor of
those that finally see print; the telltale blobs of ink and
spots of blood, sweat and tears on the paper. . . ."

It could hardly be put more eloquently.

The other morning, after reading Dr. Toro, I phoned
the Huntington Library to ask about their collection of
manuscripts, and they invited me to come out and have a
look.

Within an hour I was seated at a table in a wonderfully
quiet reading room at the Huntington with Sue Hodson,
assistant curator of literary manuscripts, looking at some of
the treasures the library has collected.

We opened a thin bound manuscript whose first page
bore the title, in small, neat handwriting:

THE RETURN OF SHERLOCK HOLMES
VII
The Adventures of the Six Napoleons

"That's Conan Doyle's original manuscript?" I asked,
feeling a bit of the thrill Professor Toro had described.

It was indeed the original, dated 1903. The story had
first appeared in *Strand* magazine the next year, after the
public had demanded their hero's return from the dead.

I began to read:

"It was no very unusual thing for Mr. Lestrade of Scot-
land Yard to look in upon us of an evening . . ."

So far so good. Then minor changes began to appear. He
had scratched out *occasion* and written in *evening*. He had
added a *very*, for emphasis. He had changed *rushing* to *hur-
rying*. He had written *They had seen a man running out of a
shop* and changed it to *They had noticed a man running out
of a shop*. (A change for the worse, if I may say so.)

He had changed *seemed to be* to *appeared to be*, for reasons known only to himself.

He had written *He lay on his back, his knees drawn up,*

and his great black beard swelling upward. . . . and changed it to *He lay on his back, his knees drawn up, and his mouth horribly open.* . . . (Indeed, a change for the better!)

He glared at us like a vicious wild beast. . . . had been changed to read *He glared at us from the shadow of his matted hair.* . . . (Ah, yes; much better, my dear Dr. Doyle.)

I wondered how many of those alterations had been due to Conan Doyle's whims of taste and how many to the urgent intrusions of Dr. Watson.

Next I found myself looking at a page of Robert Louis Stevenson's fine hand:

KIDNAPPED

"Chapter 1—I Set Off Upon My Journey to the House of Shaws."

But he hadn't liked that chapter title, so he crossed it out and wrote:

"Chapter 1—I find a Letter from the House of Shaws."

And then he begins that famous story; words I hadn't read since I was twelve:

"I will begin the story of my adventures with a certain morning . . ." But he had crossed out *a certain* and made it *April.*

Then he had crossed out *April* and restored *a certain.* Then he had gone on to write *in the month of May in the year 1749 . . .* But he had crossed out *May* and made it *June* and crossed out *1749* and made it *1751.*

At about that time, you might think, Robert Louis Stevenson would have crumpled his first page into a ball and tossed it in the wastebasket and tried some other vocation.

But no, he scribbled on. *"When I arose for the last time in my old bed . . ."* But then he crossed that out and wrote *"When I took the key for the last time out of the door of my father's house . . ."*

And so it went, page after page. And I had always admired Robert Louis Stevenson's writing because it was so

178   graceful and seemingly effortless, with an unerring choice of words.

From now on, a writer's agony will remain his secret. Nothing will remain for the archives but a letter-perfect printout and a floppy disk, from which, alas, no future historian will ever discover that his hero had feet of clay.

How to Write Real Cheese

George F. Will, a syndicated columnist of surpassing skill and erudition, wrote recently about the joy of column writing, which he calls "the perfect pleasure," and disclosed that he writes in longhand, with a fountain pen. Obviously, his manuscripts will be available to posterity.

In this age of the computer, which in one of its various functions is called a "word processor" (a term I dislike), it may seem pointlessly old-fashioned of Will to cling to longhand, though certainly it served Addison and Steele and several other of his distinguished predecessors well enough.

Also, he can hardly be called a Luddite, choosing the old ways simply out of fear and misunderstanding of the new, or he would surely still be using the quill pen and ink pot rather than the fountain pen. (Sophisticated as we are by today's advanced technology, we may wonder that the fountain pen was revolutionary when it was introduced by Mr. Waterman only a century ago.)

"I write in longhand," Will explained, "because writing should be a tactile pleasure. You should feel sentences taking shape. People who use 'word processors' should not be surprised if what they write is to real prose as processed cheese is to real cheese. . . ."

I am always meeting writers who don't know whether to buy a computer or not, and Will's disdainful warning might well decide them against it. Writers who care only about making money would be happy to turn out a product as uniform in quality and as marketable as processed cheese;

but those who have their eye on critical acclaim and the Nobel Prize may want to go on feeling their sentences taking shape.

I have been writing on a computer for two years, but before that I wrote on a typewriter as far back as my freshman year in high school. Since we built our house in Mexico, though, I have rediscovered the "tactile pleasure" of writing by hand. Though I learned penmanship in grammar school, like all good American boys of my era, I can't remember that I have ever used longhand for anything in my adult life except for taking notes, filling out forms, and writing checks.

Now, when we go down to the house on Santo Tomás Bay, I always take a couple of legal pads and a box of pencils. I keep a sharpener there. It's the only office machine in the house. When the weather is warm, I go into the back bedroom, where I have a desk, and write on a legal pad, line by line down the lined yellow paper. I keep the pencils very sharp, lining up half a dozen of them on the desk. I even enjoy the act of sharpening itself—the crunchy sound, the resistance on the crank as the blades bite into the point, the smell of the fresh wood grindings.

Of course, we have no electricity at the Baja house, but I'm sure that even if we did I wouldn't think of putting in a computer or even an electric typewriter. If I really wanted a machine, I could use a manual typewriter. At first, in fact, I took my portable down, but finally, as I say, I discovered the pleasure of writing longhand, and I am content.

I enjoy the feel as the lead point moves across the paper, looping, gliding, stopping in its tracks like a figure skater, responding to my every fancy. It is indeed a tactile pleasure.

I erase a lot, maybe giving more thought to each word than I would with a typewriter, having second thoughts and replacing some words with others. It seems to be a more deliberate process than typing.

In winter, when it's too cold in the bedroom, I sit at the dining table, warmed by the fireplace, and I am reminded of

180   Robert Louis Stevenson, whom I imagine happily scratching away with his pen in a setting much like mine.

When we get back to Los Angeles, of course, I have to transcribe what I have written—formerly to the typewritten page, now to a floppy disk.

The question is: When what I have written by longhand with such deliberation and tactile pleasure is printed finally on newsprint, having gone through my computer and the Big Computer at the *Times,* won't it come out as processed cheese?

I suppose so; but the processor that makes it processed cheese isn't the computer. It's the brain it was originally processed in.

Certainly there are reasons for writing by hand instead of by computer, but I question that a difference in the quality of the finished product is one of them. I suspect that writing is done in the mind through lightning insights and remembrances and other phenomena that no one quite understands yet, for all our fascinating research into how the brain works, and that the faster the words can be transmitted—to paper or into a computer's memory—the more likely they are to get there fresh and whole.

Of course, that is merely a theory of mine, and it, too, may be so much processed cheese.

Anyway, Will's testament to the joys and the profits of longhand certainly must reassure millions of parents who have been made to feel guilty by that television commercial in which a proud couple see their high school graduate off to college at the train station, only to meet him in shame a few weeks later when he comes home—a failure—because they never bought him a computer when he was a kid.

All any bright kid needs is a few pencils and a pencil sharpener or a fountain pen and some paper.

Accuracy, Brevity, Clarity

Meanwhile, my former colleague John Cornell wrote to express his surprise that I would use an eraser. He pointed out that Joseph Conrad and Jack London and all those fellows always crossed out words when they changed their minds (like Doyle and Stevenson) so their manuscripts would be interesting for students to pore over in museums, and he wondered how I corrected mistakes when I was a young reporter, since reporter's pencils didn't have erasers.

I answered that I simply hadn't allowed myself to make any mistakes in those days. I should have known I couldn't entirely get away with an answer like that.

Jerry Luboviski, now in sybaritic retirement, was my first editor, as editor-in-chief of the Belmont High School *Sentinel.* He also was the first to hire me after World War II, when he was city editor of the short-lived *San Diego Journal.* Again, he was briefly my city editor when we both were at the downtown *Daily News.*

"I must agree," he wrote,

> that you wrote the cleanest copy it was ever my good fortune to read. I would be less than truthful, however, if I did not note that your search for purity sometimes led to some somewhat convoluted sentences when you tried to regroup your thoughts after hitting a wrong typewriter key. . . .

I think Luboviski means that when I struck a wrong key I would try to adapt my story to the wrong letter rather than crossing it out. Say I was writing the weather story and meant to write "The sky will be clear . . ." but accidentally wrote the *ski* instead of *sky.* Rather than cross out *ski* and write *sky,* I would try to work *ski* into the story, perhaps like this:

"The weatherman predicts that the skiing will be poor,

182   since there has not been any snow on the ground in the
mountains for six months, but the sky will be clear."

Most of the time, I believe, the story was improved.

As for my writing convoluted sentences, my interpretation of a convoluted sentence being a sentence that turns in upon itself and winds itself into ever smaller and smaller circles until it vanishes in its own syntax, this obviously not being a goal of the conscientious newspaper writer, for whom the Holy Grail stands on three legs—accuracy, brevity, clarity—principles of good writing, by the way, which first were inculcated in me by none other than Jerome Luboviski himself, the Charles A. Dana of Crown Hill, on which Belmont then stood, and still does, as for my writing convoluted sentences, as I say, well, I think perhaps Luboviski, it having been a long time ago, may be exaggerating.

The outlook is for morning clouds and afternoon clear skiing.

You Can Not Make It Laugh

People who want to write better ask me whether the new computer software programs that purport to teach writing can help them.

If you write poorly, if your work is pompous, inflated, long-winded, ungrammatical and littered with misspellings, clichés, sexist words, jargon, and other careless usages, they can help.

If you write well, they can not only ruin your day; they can ruin your style.

Writing software simply analyzes something you have written, checking it against its own rigid rules of construction, diction, and syntax. It does not understand what you have written. It does not know whether your work makes sense or is engaging or dull. It has no idea whether it is artful, persuasive, banal, or inane.

The program prints out your piece, and under every line in which it finds something bad, according to its rules, it goes bingo, inserting a line that spells out your error.

The program has no ear for style; it has no common sense; it is unmoved by poetry, unconvinced by logic, unamused by humor.

You can not make it laugh; you can not make it cry; you can not make it angry. You can not even bore it.

I have just subjected an essay of mine to the scrutiny of a program called RIGHTWRITER. Its purpose and method are described in the manual:

"RIGHTWRITER is a writing aid to help you create strong clear documents. The program uses advanced artificial intelligence techniques to analyze a document. . . ."

It admits its limitations: "RIGHTWRITER does not understand the meaning of words, nor does it understand the exercise of literary license."

Consequently, it may mark correct or allowable usages as errors. It is to be used only as a guide, not a final authority.

One thing RIGHTWRITER hates (without feeling, of course) is sentences that are more than twenty-two words long. It also hates uncommon words, complex sentences, sentences starting with "But," and the passive voice.

In my brief piece (930 words) RIGHTWRITER found 13 sentences of more than 22 words each, 5 complex sentences, 5 uses of the passive voice, 3 sentences beginning with "But," and 23 uncommon words.

RIGHTWRITER summarized that I had a readability index of 8.4 (readers would need an eighth-grade level of education to understand me); a strength index of 0.41 (on a scale of 0.0 to 1.0); a descriptive index (the use of adjectives and adverbs) of 0.54 (within the normal range).

Its recommendations: "The writing can be made more direct by using the active voice. . . ." (Does *writing* use the active voice? Or does the *writer?*) "Try to use more simple sentences. . . ."

184   Evidently it wants me to get my work down to the fourth-grade level.

RIGHTWRITER also printed out a list of all the "uncommon" words I used. Among them were such uncommon words as *gadgets, incoming, plates, vanity, byline, gimmicks, push buttons, religious, therapy, wisdom, fashionable, hula,* and *theoretically.*

Here's an example of one of my worst sentences:

"The personalized number is seen as a blessing for single people, who can give it to people they hope to hear from, and since the number theoretically will be easier to remember, perhaps they will get more calls."

Not only is that sentence too long, having thirty-eight words in it, but it is also too complex, having three commas; it contains a passive verb *(is seen)* and an uncommon word *(theoretically).*

Here's another:

"But if all you can find out is the number the call came from, it won't help you much unless you know whose number that is. Of course, if the call was from a member of your family or a close friend or your employer, you will know the number, and you can call back."

Both those sentences are too long for RIGHTWRITER; the second one is complex, and the first one begins with "But."

I wonder what RIGHTWRITER would say about Thomas Jefferson's Declaration of Independence. This great document, from which our blessed freedom springs, begins with a sentence of seventy-one words, and the sixth sentence begins with "But"!

(That last sentence of mine, by the way, not only has an interior clause but also ends with an exclamation point, both of which RIGHTWRITER frowns on.

What would RIGHTWRITER say of Jefferson's uncommon words, such as *unalienable, transient, usurpations, evinces, constrains, inestimable, annihilation, perfidy, magnanimity,* and others?

I have been rereading John Steinbeck's *Cannery Row,*

and I find that the first sentence is twenty-five words long and the second is forty-two.

Of course, RIGHTWRITER is not designed to analyze historical documents or works of genius. It is meant only to improve the writing of ordinary contemporaries.

I don't mean to compare myself with Jefferson or Steinbeck, but I think they prove that a sentence need not be short to be clear and that a long sentence, if its structure is good, can convey more than a series of short sentences of the kind that RIGHTWRITER evidently approves of, it being more forceful to use a long word that says exactly what one means to say than a short word that everyone knows but which is less precise, because if you write constantly for readers at the fourth-grade level, you are not likely to be engaging the interest of more educated readers, and if we cannot entertain the educated, what is the point of writing, since the object of the written word is to convey information and express ideas and to extend the limits of our understanding!

But that, it must be confessed, is only my opinion.

SUBJECT A

Is Sex Leisure?

According to the preliminary findings of a twenty-year study of leisure, Americans have less of it than the Dutch, the Danes, the Canadians, and the British. And the French, believe it or not, have less than any other people in the eleven Western states.

These improbable figures were reported by *Los Angeles Times* staff writer Betty Cuniberti from the work of sociology professor John Robinson at the University of Maryland.

Professor Robinson makes a basic error, I believe, in his definition of leisure. First, he does not consider eating as a leisure occupation. That is obviously how the French managed to score last. Anyone who has ever been in France knows that the French spend most of their leisure time in shopping for meals, preparing meals, and eating meals.

Naturally, since preparing meals is a French housewife's vocation, she may not consider it leisure; but certainly the prolonged time spent at table, both at lunch and dinner, is the only social life she has and must be considered as leisure even if she has to wash the dishes afterward.

Considering the amount of time that French people spend eating and drinking, I am amazed that television has caught on in that country at all. However, we may have discovered the explanation one day when we had lunch with

187

188   a French couple at their rural house in the Pyrenees. Throughout the entire meal, a television set remained on, within full view of the table, and with the sound turned up. Still, no one watched it.

I think that proves that given a choice between television and lunch, the French will take lunch; and it implies that in France eating is an act of leisure.

I think Professor Robinson was also naive, and perhaps a bit Puritan, when he declined to place sex in the leisure category. The professor explains that he did not wish to pry into the privacy of his subjects, so he arbitrarily assigned sex to "personal care," as if it were no more enjoyable than taking a shower, brushing one's teeth, or grooming one's hair.

If Professor Robinson had put sex where it belongs, in leisure, we might have found out whether the amount of time most human beings spend on it has been reduced by television.

On the other hand, categorizing sex as a leisure-time activity might not have altered Professor Robinson's findings as to the relative amount of leisure time enjoyed overall by various nationalities. Since sex, like eating lunch, may be indulged in while the television set is left running, the amount of time spent on it might then have been disguised as watching TV.

Probably television has made greater intrusions on other activities, such as household chores and child rearing, than on sex and eating.

A recent *New Yorker* cartoon shows a young mother and father sitting on a couch in front of the tube, mesmerized, while their infant toddles down the hallway crying, "I'm walking!"

Had it not been for the magnetism of TV, these parents very likely would have been engaged in helping their child to take its first steps instead of watching a soap opera about "real life."

Professor Robinson has some trouble with his finding that employed American women have only nineteen hours of free time a week, while men have twenty-two. However, he noted, when employed women and housewives are taken together, they have about the same amount of leisure time as employed men.

Once again, I think it may be a question of categories, as with sex. When a man spends three hours watching a football game, he is obviously at leisure. At the same time, his wife may be luxuriating in her bath, doing her hair, painting her toenails, and otherwise enjoying herself. Yet this is not considered leisure.

I notice that Professor Robinson has also assigned the time spent commuting between home and work as "contracted time," or work time.

On the contrary, the time spent on the freeway driving to and from work is the most precious leisure time some of us have. For once in the day, we are alone. We are free to contemplate life, to think about truth, to listen to the unforgettables on KMPC or to Michael Jackson on KABC.

Unless we are upwardly mobile enough to have a car telephone, nobody can reach us. We are encapsulated, isolated from the demands of our world in our mobile container.

Cuniberti didn't say whether Professor Robinson categorized aerobic and isometric exercise as work or leisure. He would probably call it leisure, but when I see these young and not as young pushing, pulling, puffing, straining, and sweating, it looks like work to me.

If people can spend an hour or two every day pumping iron and riding stationary bicycles, they have too much leisure, and society has failed.

Don't they know they could be reading, eating, having sex, or watching television?

LaLaLanD

190 ## Is Sex Necessary?

We have been told recently, in numerous alarming magazine articles and surveys, that the contemporary male is reluctant to commit himself to marriage, or any lasting relationship with a woman, and that women, consequently, especially if they are older than thirty, have scant chance of finding a suitable mate, much less of going to the altar.

No one seems to know quite how to explain this depressing phenomenon or what to do about it, although our society is not without an abundance of psychologists, psychiatrists, sex counselors, advice columnists, and call-in radio-show hosts, Oprah, Phil, Sally Jesse, and, of course, Geraldo.

Actually, this problem was treated with remarkable insight and prescience by the late James Thurber and E. B. White in their little book *Is Sex Necessary?* which was first published in 1929. Although Thurber and White speak of being in a "sexual revolution," they obviously had experienced only the preliminary feminist wave of the 1920s and not the far more revolutionary women's movement of the 1960s, including the Pill.

Even so, they seemed to understand our sexual dilemma and to put their fingers on it in the lucid prose for which both are so admired. (I suspect, however, that Thurber wrote this book, though White contributed a perceptive footnote on Thurber's drawings, and there is a ripping preface by Lt. Col. H. R. L. Le Boutellier, C.I.E., of Schlaugenschloss Haus, King's Byway, Boissy-Le-Doux sur Seine.)

Colonel Le Boutellier (who sounds suspiciously like Thurber) traces the problem back to the primeval soup:

> Men and woman have always sought, by one means and another, to be together rather than apart. At first they were together by the simple expedient of being unicellular, and there was no conflict. Later

the cell separated, or began living apart, for reasons which are not clear even today. . . . Almost immediately the two halves of the original cell began experiencing a desire to unite again—usually with a half of some other cell. This urge has survived down to our time. Its commonest manifestations are marriage, divorce, neuroses, and, a little less frequently, gunfire. . . .

The authors find the root of the problem in the American concern with the psyche in sex.

The American idea is to point out, first of all, the great and beautiful part which the stars, and the infinite generally, play in man's relationship to women. The French, Dutch, Brazilians, Danes, etc., can proceed in their amours on a basis entirely divorced from the psyche.

They suggest that sex has been destroyed by books on sex. For example, a young man who doesn't know whether what he feels for a young woman is love or passion consults a book on sexology and finds, in a chapter on "The Theory of the Libido," the following:

The ideal healthy outcome is to find the child in whom the process of repression has been accomplished with no fixations of interest at lower stages of adaptation, in whom the Oedipus complex has passed into a "normal" phase of the castration complex inhibition, and in whom a free-moving libido is developing sublimation in active interests free from paralyzing inhibitions or anti-social tendencies.

Confronted with this alarming analysis, the young man flees to Oregon, "where he raises fruit fairly successfully and with no anti-social tendencies."

The authors hold that sex and marriage in the nine-

192   teenth century were economic and patriotic; we needed
children to build the nation. There was no psychic element.
"There was not a single case of nervous breakdown, or neurosis, arising from amatory troubles, in the whole cycle from
1800 to 1900, barring a slight flareup just before the Mexican and Civil wars. . . ."

They place part of the blame for the alienation of their
times on "pedestalism," the emerging tendency of men to
place woman on a pedestal, to think of her as ineffable, an
unattainable deity, something too precious to be touched.
Awed by this vision, men withdrew to their dens.

In the early part of this century, they hold, women discovered their "right to be sexual," and they "fell to with a
will."

It was this change, they suggest, that caused the problem we are hearing about today.

> The transition from amiability to sexuality was revo-
> lutionary. It presented a terrific problem to Woman,
> because in acquiring and assuming the habits that
> tended to give her an equality with Man, she discov-
> ered that she necessarily became a good deal like
> Man. The more she got like him, the less he saw in
> her. (Or so he liked to think, anyway.)

I'm afraid that White and Thurber's thesis on the mas-
culinization of women would be anathematized today as
sexist, which indeed it is. Why cannot a woman be sexually
aggressive and remain feminine? Still, there may be some
validity in their notion that it is our concern with the
psychic aspects of our sexual relationships that makes them
so difficult to maintain.

This book offers no answers to the dilemmas it describes,
but if the reader seeks guidance, I recommend him to
Thurber's later book, *Let Your Mind Alone!* in which he
conjures up a pox on all the how-to books, which first began
to burgeon in that era.

"Man will be better off," he said, "if he quits monkeying with his mind and just lets it alone."

It's something to think about.

Here's to the Girl Next Door

"Psychologists say" is a pop phrase of our times that is most often encountered in newspapers, where it introduces some new and often poppycockful explanation of contemporary behavior. Psychologists always come forth, for example, to explain the "psychology" of the latest multiple killer, though of course no scientific study of multiple killers has been made.

What psychologists say is often based on some funded study of the subject, but it may also merely be a theory thought up in the quiet of the psychologist's study. I have an idea that psychologists, like any other kind of professionals, are eager to practice their specialty once they get their degrees. They hang up their shingles and begin to make pronouncements on the motivations of their fellow beings, much as a dentist hangs up his shingle and begins to pull teeth.

In this age of science and information we are eager to know everything, and I do not blame psychologists for taking a shot at explaining us to ourselves. I have an idea they are right about as often as medical doctors, political analysts, and theoretical physicists.

Nothing should lie outside fair inquiry. If psychologists want to find out whether there is a scientific basis for the notion that gentlemen prefer blondes, more power to them. If they want to find out whether redheads are better lovers, let them go to it.

I did not even object to that funded study made a few years ago at UCLA in which psychologists tried to find out, by laboratory tests, whether so-called conversation pieces actually stimulated conversation, even though the result

194 seemed predictable. They found that it depends on the conversation piece and the people engaged in the conversation.

Now I read in a syndicated column by Maxwell Glen and Cody Shearer that psychologists say the gorgeous women shown in television, in magazine ads, on billboards, and in such soft-porn magazines as *Playboy* and *Penthouse* are inhibiting the sex lives of young American men. According to Glen and Shearer, the young men's expectations of female beauty are so fantastically elevated by the young women they see displayed that no woman they actually meet and get acquainted with can possibly come up to those heights.

"Welcome to America's latest neurosis," they say: "The unrealistic expectations of the American male."

They quote Douglas T. Kenrick, psychologist at Arizona State University, whose research "has confirmed what other psychologists have discovered"—that men subjected to the kind of female sexuality and beauty exploited by Madison Avenue are so far beyond the reality of everyday life that men are disappointed and dissatisfied by ordinary women.

"Accordingly," the columnists say, "there is not enough healthy interaction between the sexes."

They say this phenomenon is causing men to delay marriage.

Somehow I'm not too worried about this latest finding of psychologists. Young men in America have been exposed to the glamour girls of motion pictures and advertising for a good many decades, and yet they managed to have school and office romances and to get married and have children and sometimes even to be in love.

That all the young men of my generation were in love with June Allyson and Carole Lombard and Ingrid Bergman didn't mean that we were incapable of falling for the girls we took to their movies. Actually, I found a girl that was prettier than any of them, and I convinced her that I wasn't unworthy of her hand.

On several occasions in recent years I have visited high

school and college campuses, and I want to tell you that the girls are as pretty as ever, and there is no chance that young men are going to fall on their swords, so to speak, because they can't have Miss Centerfold.

It is possible, as Kenrich says, that many young men have an idealized vision of their own beauty and thus find it hard to meet their match. There is nothing new in male vanity; it preceded the movies, advertising, and TV, but it has never protected men against the natural seductiveness of ordinary young women.

If there were any truth in Kenrick's analysis, I should think it would apply to women's view of men as well as vice versa. How about all the handsome young men in the movies and TV, all those rough-hewn types in the beer ads, for example? Don't young woman look at those hunks and then look around them and say, "Hey, aren't there any good-looking guys in real life?"

Not a chance.

Remember that movie *Marty* where Ernest Borgnine, who wasn't too much to look at, fell in love with a woman who wasn't too much to look at, either?

I believe there's a guy for every girl, and vice versa, and *Playboy* and *Playgirl* magazines aren't going to make it any different.

Here's to the girl next door.

Whatever Became of the Cute Meet?

I have received a letter addressed "Occupant" from a company called Great Expectations inviting me to find my ideal mate through their video viewing service.

"It's sad but true," the letter begins. "So many of us never find the one ideal, fully satisfying relationship of our dreams."

196 I don't know how our address got on their list, but I want to advise Great Expectations that I am not in the market for a new ideal mate. I already have my ideal mate.

I suppose such computer errors are easy to understand. I know people whose *dogs* have received letters inviting them to invest in mutual funds or life insurance. So I'm not offended. But I'm not sure that video viewing is the most romantic path to an ideal relationship.

The letter asks me to fill out a questionnaire about myself and also about the kind of ideal mate I'm seeking. Then, evidently, I will be interviewed on videotape and will be able to screen their videotape file of female applicants.

Perhaps I should not assume that Great Expectations is limited to male-female relationships. But the questions do not seem to include any other kind.

"Great Expectations offers you a better way that has helped thousands of discriminating couples to meet and fall in love," the letter says. 'Our selective Video Viewing Service lets you screen, at your leisure, our extensive videotape library of attractive, eligible singles. Viewing in relaxed privacy, you see and hear them in natural interviews . . . then, select whom you'd like to meet."

That does sound better than sitting around in a crowded singles bar, boozing and breathing smoke and being elbowed by six-foot-four-inch iron pumpers.

Still, I wonder whatever became of the old-fashioned cute meet. The cute meet was a story device much favored by screenwriters of the 1930s and 1940s. Boy meets girl by accident. Boy and girl fall in love. Then the complications; for a time boy would lose girl. But in the end boy won girl, and we all left the theater happy.

They could meet at the museum, standing together in front of a Matisse. He might say, "That girl's arm is too long." And she might say (as Matisse once did), "That's not a girl, that's a painting."

Bingo. They're in love.

Or they might get on a streetcar together on a rainy

day. He would zip up his raincoat and catch her sleeve in the zipper. She would be annoyed at first; and then they would begin to laugh. Zowie! Love at first sight.

Or she's at Trader Joe's looking for a bottle of red wine to serve with her boeuf bourguignon at the little dinner she's preparing for her boss. He notices her indecision. "Have you tried the Gallo?" he says, looking into her eyes and quoting James Thurber: "It's a native domestic Burgundy without any breeding, but I think you'll be amused by its presumption."

She looks into his eyes. The boss is forgotten. Two souls are mated.

Or she's working at the china counter in the five-and-ten-cent store. He ducks into the store to get out of the rain. The rain continues for an hour. He keeps buying china. Result: a little penthouse for two, where they'll always contrive to keep love and romance forever alive.

Or he turns up at a small apartment he's rented in New York. But she's rented it first, and she's in it. It's the only apartment left in town. He prevails upon her to let him share it. They hang up a sheet as a partition. You know how that one turns out.

Or she's a missionary's spinster sister in Africa, and he's a drunken riverboat captain. They are driven together by a German raid and escape in his boat. At first she is frightened of him and repulsed by his dissolute character. But several harrowing episodes later and after her glorious awakening— wedding bells!

What would life be without those cute meets? Without the hope, however small, that every day one goes out into the city or into a supermarket or gets on a bus or an airplane or crosses a street, one may encounter one's true love in the guise of a stranger?

"The ideal mate of your dreams, whom you might otherwise never meet," says Great Expectations, "is most likely waiting for you in our Video Library, right now."

If I weren't already mated for life, I don't think I'd

198   want to sit in somebody's video library and run through a
pile of videotapes in search of my ideal.

I certainly don't mean to discourage anyone else from
trying it. I'm sure there are thousands of singles in our cities
who despair of ever meeting anyone suitable and will try
almost anything, including the preparation of little dinners
for their bosses.

But if I were single, I'd head for the museum and keep
my eyes open.

THE GREAT AMERICAN SPORT

Baseball Is Sacred

A reader has sent me a copy of a letter he wrote to Peter Ueberroth, commissioner of baseball, suggesting that the rules of the game be changed so that a batter who has hit a home run does not have to run the bases.

"After a batter has hit a home run," argues Jerry Nashel of Pasadena, "it appears of no practical purpose for him to be required to touch each base and finally home plate. . . .

"A home run is a home run. Why this ritualistic jog of seemingly no practical value? I would like to propose that the hitter have the option to jog the base paths if he chooses, and still have the run count if he chooses not to. . . ."

I am not a sportswriter; baseball is religious in form, and sportswriters are its high priests. But baseball belongs to all Americans. Its rites are sacred and not to be trifled with. They must be protected by us laymen.

It is true, as Nashel says, that once a home run has been hit, no practical purpose is served by having the batter run the bases. The ball is unplayable. The batter himself, and any runners on base at the time, are home free, so to speak.

What would he have them do? Leave their bases and trot across the field to their dugout? Does he want the bat-

200   ter himself merely to turn from the batter's box, tip his cap
to the crowd, and then withdraw?

Never. The drama of the home run does not end with
the disappearance of the ball in the bleachers. We want to
see each runner tagging each base, we want to count the
runs as each runner crosses the plate; we want, mainly, to
see the triumphant strut of the batter, the hero, as he
rounds first base, knowing already that he has done it, then
raises a clenched fist or doffs his cap as he takes the other
bases in an exuberant gallop while the crowd roars.

Is it possible that Nashel is too young ever to have seen
a newsreel of Babe Ruth rounding the bases, tipping his cap
to the multitudes, after belting one out of Yankee Stadium?
Does he not remember the Babe's comical look, a football
on toothpicks, as he made his ritualistic circuit?

Could he have missed the home run hit by Bill Mazeroski in the bottom of the ninth inning of the seventh game
of the World Series between the Pirates and the Yankees in
1960? Mazeroski's homer came with the score tied 9–9, and
he went around the bases in a series of joyful leaps, like a
gazelle, while the Pirate crowd went out of its mind.

What would he have wanted Mazeroski to do? Lean on
his bat and take a bow?

And what about Kirk Gibson's historic pinch homer in
the bottom of the ninth in the first game of the 1988 World
Series? Gibson hobbles out of the dugout on two crippled
legs to pinch hit with one on, two out, the Dodgers trailing
the Oakland A's 4–3. On the full count—three balls and two
strikes—Gibson belts one over the right-field wall and then
limps around the bases, clenched fists raised, while 55,983
Dodger fans rend the skies.

What fan would want to be denied that heroic run?

Nashel might as well propose that pitchers simply wave
batters to first base when they want to walk them instead of
throwing four straight balls out of reach.

Surely the intentional walk is the most ritualistic and
meaningless act in baseball. Imagine the time and boredom
that would be saved if the pitcher could nod the batter on

and save those pitchouts. But that wouldn't be baseball.
Who knows? The pitcher might carelessly throw one the
batter can reach and give up a homer. Besides, the batter is
entitled to those four pitched balls.

If he is so good that the pitcher is afraid to pitch to him,
why should the pitcher be able to avoid those extra pitches,
which theoretically won't do his arm any good?

Besides, the deliberate base on balls gives the crowd a
moment to stretch and get some peanuts.

If Nashel wants to change the rules, how about dumping
the designated-hitter rule? This silly business (in the American League only, so far) allows a manager to designate a
batter to bat for the pitcher, throughout the game. Thus,
pitchers, who are notoriously poor batters, don't have to
bat.

Remember Don Drysdale? Don hit 29 home runs in his
career and had a batting average of .186. Does that sound
like an automatic out?

Who wants to see a designated hitter bat for Fernando
Valenzuela? Fernando is always dangerous at the plate, and
with a team like the Dodgers behind him, he sometimes has
to bat to win his own games.

Baseball is an old, beautiful chesslike game. Its rules
have been worked out to mathematical perfection. It takes
a fast batter almost exactly the time to get to first base as it
takes a good third baseman to field a well-hit ground ball
and throw to first. A good runner can get from second base
to home on a single to center field. Maybe. It depends on
how fast he is and who's in center field.

Baseball is sacred, and any change is sacrilege.

Casey at the Bat

Our eight-year-old grandson Casey stayed at our house a
few days while he was attending the Manny Mota Baseball

202   Camp at Scholl Canyon Playground, in the hills above
        Glendale.

        He was my responsibility, man to man.

        The camp started at nine o'clock on a Monday morning.
        The playground has three baseball diamonds and a green
        field on a plateau high in the hills. It is surrounded by euca-
        lyptus trees. To the south the spires of the downtown sky-
        line arise from the smog.

        We stood in line to register. There were about thirty
        boys. As they signed in, the man gave each a blue T-shirt
        with a picture of Manny Mota on it and the words "Manny
        Mota Baseball Camp."

        A stocky man in T-shirt, shorts, and a baseball cap gave
        a talk about the camp. He sounded sharp, firm, and gentle.
        He said, "I'm Coach Paul," and nodding toward a young
        man at his side, "This is Coach Gary."

        Coach Paul said every boy would have to wear an ath-
        letic supporter and a cup because of the danger of injury.
        "Not today," he said. "We'll take it easy today. But tomor-
        row."

        The two coaches and two assistants led the boys out to
        the green field and formed them into two groups according
        to age: seven, eight, nine and ten-year-olds; and eleven-year-
        olds and older.

        All of a sudden Manny Mota himself was standing out
        in front of them like a knight in his white Dodger uniform
        with the big *11* on back. He gave them a talk.

        Then the coaches lined them up and made them do cal-
        isthenics. This was the hard part. It reminded me of boot
        camp. The coach explained that the exercises were to limber
        them up so they wouldn't get hurt.

        "What you learn here," he said, "will help you prevent
        injury all the way up to the pros."

        It was out. The magic word. The impossible dream. The
        pros. There was always a chance. You might make it, even
        though the odds were about 100,000 to 1.

        Coach Paul made them do two laps. They were soon
        straggled out, with the little guys far in the rear.

Then the boys paired up and began playing catch with their partners. The older boys threw harder, faster, more accurately, and with the easy athletic grace that most boys achieve in their teens. Life is unfair.

Mota came off the field and slapped hands with the few parents who were still standing around. He had charisma, and he knew that it was important to spread it around.

Manuel Rafael Geronimo (Manny) Mota, out of Santo Domingo, played twenty years in the major leagues, twelve years with the Dodgers. Lifetime batting average: .304. In three league championship series he got three pinch hits in five at bats.

I went home, satisfied that my grandson was in good hands. I phoned his father and asked him if Casey had a jockstrap.

"A jockstrap!" He laughed. "Does he need one? I didn't have one until I was in high school."

I went to a Big 5 in Glendale and asked a young clerk if they had jockstraps and cups. "I need a very small size," I said.

He raised an eyebrow.

"It's not for me," I said.

We picked out one, with plastic cup, that was labeled Young/Small.

I went back to the park about two o'clock. Casey's group was at batting practice, half lined up to bat, half out in the field with their gloves on. Casey was in line to bat. Coach Paul would toss the ball toward the plate from the side, and the batter would swing at it. Sometimes he missed the ball entirely, just like Pedro Guerrero.

Casey came up. He swung at the first ball and missed. He swung again and missed. Manny Mota himself, now wearing a Manny Mota Baseball Camp T-shirt, walked over and moved Casey's feet. Just so. He told him how to hold the bat, how to keep his elbows in.

"Keep your eye on the ball!" he exhorted.

The next ball Casey belted over second base. He obviously had been metamorphosed by that laying on of hands.

204

Before dinner we played a game he had brought from home. It depended purely on luck, and he beat me. "Haven't you got any games that require skill?" I asked.

He got a word game out of his satchel. It was a circular box in which nine letters were displayed at random. Each of us wrote down whatever words of four letters or more we could make of those nine letters.

The first group of letters was *g, x, c, y, d, e, r, b, e*. A few minutes later I had ten words: *bred, reed, deer, gyre, beer, cede, reedy, creed, dreg, breed*. He had *reed, deer, and beer*. He challenged *gyre, cede, creed,* and *dreg*, but we looked them up in the dictionary, and he conceded.

I think it's important to remind them that you know more than they do.

"How about Scrabble?" he said. I agreed. He won 57–30.

When my wife came home, I told her about the athletic supporter. "Do you want to show him how to put it on?" I asked.

"No," she said. "That's your job."

I asked him, "Do you know what a jockstrap is?"

He shook his head.

I told him what the jockstrap and the cup were for and how to put them on.

It was a rite of passage for us both.

What's Wrong in Albuquerque?

According to a survey published in a recent issue of *Forbes*, Los Angeles is one of the four worst American cities for happy marriages.

The other three are New York, Washington, and, improbably, Albuquerque.

The four best cities are Philadelphia, Pittsburgh, Cleveland, and Orlando, Florida.

Orlando is easy enough to understand. It is populated

mostly by older couples whose marriages are long since past the crisis point. A marriage based on community life savings and Social Security is relatively safe.

I have no idea what makes marriages last longer in Philadelphia, Pittsburgh, and Cleveland. If we can believe our myths, Pittsburgh and Cleveland are capitals of banality, and Philadelphia is ruled by an encrusted elite and a corrupt bureaucracy.

Perhaps banality is good for a marriage. Without the excitements and distractions of the more sophisticated cities, the old Good Housekeeping values may prevail.

I have always had the perhaps naive idea that a city with a first-class symphony orchestra and a major league baseball team was a good place to live and raise a family.

Cleveland and Philadelphia have first-class orchestras, and I imagine that Pittsburgh has, too, though I've never heard it. Also, all three have major league baseball teams, so it should be no surprise that their homes are happy, their marriages stable.

This standard fails, however, when you consider that Los Angeles and New York both have world-class symphonies and major league baseball teams, yet their marriages are said to be in disarray.

Washington's problem is easier to understand. The loss of that city's major league baseball franchise may indeed have shattered its marital equilibrium. Without its beloved Senators, Washington is a city of unrequited love; a child that has lost its teddy bear.

I have no doubt that Washington's marriages would revive if its baseball franchise were restored. A big city without a baseball team has no heart, no core, no reason for being. What chance has a marriage without its spring hopes, its winning streaks, its shutouts, its hits, its runs, its errors, without a baseball team to serve as a metaphor, to resonate to its wins and losses?

Still, both the Los Angeles and New York franchises prosper. Why, then, are those two cities so inhospitable to married life?

206   According to the survey, "In New York married couples have time for everything but each other and become two people passing in the kitchen."

That may be true. Everything is so accessible in New York. All those little delis and art galleries. The bars, the park, the zoo, the museums, the subways rushing here and there, the off-Broadway theaters, the shops, the teeming sidewalks. So much to do. Inevitably, marriages collapse in the kitchens of tiny apartments just as their partners do.

I have an idea that if New York couples went to the symphony once a week in winter and to the ballpark once a week in summer, their marriages would last.

"In Los Angeles," the survey said, "everybody is eyeing everybody else. Too many beautiful distractions."

I suggest the same antidote. The music hall and the ballpark are public places. People are thrown together. But I doubt that any adulteries ever started in one or the other. One concentrates either on the conductor's baton or the batter's bat: one is not susceptible to the meaningful glance, the lingering handclasp.

Coincidentally, I happened to be in Albuquerque when I read about the *Forbes* report in a newspaper. My wife and I had just driven through the city, and it seemed to be, if there is any such thing left in America today, a pretty, medium-sized, stable, prosperous, healthful place to live.

It was smaller than I would have thought, and older, with thousands of houses from the first half of the century enclosing a downtown that is rising from its ruins: a downtown of medium-height, new buildings done in the pervasive southwestern style, looking vaguely like Aztec temples.

A handsome mall had been cut straight through these ornaments, wide and refreshing, with a gushing fountain at its center and a handsome new library on one corner.

It seemed to be a city in which people were trying. I had no doubt that its women were busy behind the scenes in restoration and cultural work, supporting schools, libraries, and their symphony orchestra. (It was doing excerpts from

Aida, Il Trovatore, and *La Forza del Destino* while we were there.)

What, unhappy? According to the survey, it was the worst of cities for marriage: "Managers (the ones consulted in the survey) feel isolated from its Wild West culture, and notice an undercurrent of rebellion among the children."

I don't know why children would rebel against a Wild West culture, but I can see that women might. There are still a lot of Carol Kennicotts in mid-America, frustrated by insularity, cultural hunger, and the lack of a major league baseball team.

As we flew over the city on our way home, I looked down in vain for some sign of dismembered homes, anguished wives, disgruntled husbands, and rebellious children.

They have their symphony, and they have a Triple A baseball team. What more can they ask for starters?

SEX IN THE MOVIES

A Kiss Was Just a Kiss

Something has happened to kissing in the movies, and, I would guess, in real life, too, since all our manners and morals are taken from the movies.

When I was young and a rather active kisser, one simply placed one's lips on those of one's enamorata, or target, and held them there for a moment or two, the amount of pressure and the length of time depending on one's earnestness and ultimate intentions.

One then withdrew and appraised one's reactions as well as those of one's partner. If there was a certain breathlessness, a kind of swirling of the senses, a warmth that spread to one's loins and toes, then it was a serious kiss, and it was up to the young woman, or girl, as we called her then, whether she wanted to do it again and risk even further complications.

Sometimes a kiss was merely a brief touching of the lips, a brushing, with no pressure and no lingering, and even this light contact could produce literally staggering results.

Do you remember those old movies in which Cary Grant would kiss Rosalind Russell, for the first time, briefly and tenderly, and Miss Russell would push herself away, crossing her eyes, gasping for breath and reeling slightly, like an animal stunned by a tranquilizing dart; and everyone in the

210   audience would know, along with Miss Russell, that something important had happened?

Even such forceful he-men as Clark Gable and Errol Flynn kissed their ladies rather lightly, leaving it to their mysterious male magnetism or electricity, or whatever it was, to soften, stimulate, and seduce.

Sometimes the male showed his physical superiority by clutching the female in his arms and bending her over backward, so that she was supposedly helpless, as he planted his mesmerizing kiss on her flattened lips.

All these heroines had to do, if they wished to resist, was bite their oppressor on his lower lip; but somehow that never occurred to them. Or perhaps there is some essence in a kiss, like the poison extruded by certain insects and reptiles, that momentarily paralyzes its victims.

But that kind of kissing is gone, as dead as the Hays Production Code, which once forbade movies to show the inside of a woman's thigh, much less her naked breast, and even dictated that a man and a woman could not be shown in bed together unless they were married and had their clothes on and the beds were twins.

Alas, that sort of kiss, in which closed lips were pressed together, has gone from the screen except between cousins and closer relatives. It has been replaced by what is known as the open-mouth kiss. We know it is called an "open-mouth kiss" because 'lustful and open-mouth kissing" was banned by the Hays Office in 1930.

In the open-mouth kiss, the man and woman meet with mouths wide open, as if they were licking candied apples. Now and then one sees a tongue arching out toward the opposite opening, in which it is at once enclosed. One has no doubt that this practice is reciprocal and that the tongue thus extruded quickly retreats to allow the entry of its opposite number.

In a really all-out open-mouth kiss the two lovers (can anyone doubt that that is what they are or soon will be?) resemble creatures of the primeval swamp attempting to swallow one another.

Mind, I am not against this sort of exercise. I'm sure it is effective in arousing both partners and allows them to dispense with a lot of sparring and idle conversation.

Indeed, we had a milder version of the open kiss when I was in high school. It was known as a French kiss. In this amorous adventure one partner darted the tip of his tongue into the other's mouth, and vice versa. Their lips appeared to remain closed, however, and a casual observer would not have guessed that a tantalizing exchange of tongues was taking place. But the French kiss was not universally practiced, and a girl who permitted it, or worse, initiated it, was regarded as fast, if not lost.

Movies were so pure, however, that even the French kiss was not permitted, so far as we knew. But I have learned from *The Book of Kisses* (Dembner Books), by Danny Biederman, that actresses of that era were always complaining about the illegal kissing of their leading men. Evidently some of our heroes ignored the Hays Office rules.

As late as 1950, according to Biederman, Kathryn Grayson complained that Mario Lanza "not only kept trying to stuff his tongue down my throat, but he kept eating garlic for lunch," and Olivia de Havilland complained that in *My Cousin Rachel* Richard Burton "had his tongue down my mouth right there in front of the camera."

I guess those fellows were just ahead of their times.

Gone with the Wind

"The way some movies are described," writes Joan Colgrove, "is most intriguing. What does 'adult language' mean? And the really baffling term, 'mild violence'? Is that when someone is snuffed by a .44 magnum instead of being torn apart by a pack of wolves . . . ?"

She is referring to the brief reviews of movies in the program magazines received by subscribers to HBO, Z, and other pay-TV channels.

212   I know what she means. I get two of those magazines, and I always read the reviews they offer to discriminating viewers who need guidance in deciding whether to watch such features as *Rumble Fish, Throne of Blood, Creepshow,* and *Porky's.*

I don't envy the people who write them. It can't be easy to convey the essence of such movies in a few words, especially when some of them obviously have few redeeming qualities, if any.

As for the ambiguous labels that trouble Colgrove, I don't think they should be blamed so much on those critics as on the motion-picture rating code under which movies that aren't considered 100 percent wholesome are categorized as X, R, PG, or PG-13—the X meaning sexually explicit, the R meaning not for children under seventeen, the PG standing for "parental guidance" (whatever that means) of children under seventeen, and PG-13, the same for children under thirteen.

I have never understood how parents who presumably have not seen a movie themselves are to exercise guidance on it. I have an idea that parents who are strict won't let them see it; parents who are liberal will; and most won't pay any attention.

I was a good friend of Dick Mathison, who was for several years a member of the board that rates movies. He once sighed to me when we were having a beer at the Cock 'n' Bull, to which the stress of his office often drove him, "I wonder if a movie *can* hurt children."

My feeling is that if movies do hurt children, it is not because of sex, violence, or "adult language" but because of the way they make them seem heroic and glamorous, along with greed, larceny, and bad table manners.

"Adult language" means that there is some use, or more likely a lot, of words that used to be taboo not only in the movies but also in polite company. In this usage, *adult* means *obscene.* If the word is used of a book, or of a movie as a whole, it means *pornographic.* Thus, the word has become almost useless in the sense of *mature*. An adult person. An adult attitude. Adult conversation. All obsolete.

Presumably, if I were to say that I had engaged in an adult conversation with a dean of the Harvard Law School, you might not know whether we had talked about a new Supreme Court decision or the 101 positions of the Kamasutra.

Good-bye *adult*. It has gone forever, like *gay*, which will never be gay again.

As for "mild violence," I hardly know what that could be. As Colgrove suggests, it must be when someone is merely snuffed out with a .44 Magnum. A .44 Magnum bullet will make a large hole in the human breast and an enormous hole at the exit; but that is, indeed, mild violence compared to what we often see these days.

I remember when violence was mostly accomplished off-screen. The worst it ever got on-screen was in those marathon fistfights between heroes like John Wayne and Victor McLaglen; mighty blows they struck, giving and absorbing them far beyond the limits of human endurance, yet never a blow was struck. Violence was when James Cagney ground half a grapefruit in Mae Clarke's face. The audience gasped. It was too cruel. Everyone who saw that scene remembers it to this day.

So "mild violence" in today's movies is something so bloody, so ghastly that if you were to witness it in real life, you would remember it forever; and if you were a small child, you might be damaged by it in some permanent way. But seeing it in today's movies, which have regressed us to the Middle Ages, it will seem merely routine and is not likely to do children as much damage as trick-or-treat candy.

I don't remember what the adjective is for violence that is worse than mild, but probably there is none. The language falters.

A common explanation of an R rating of the cable reviews is "sexual situations," which is superior to "adult language" and "mild violence," I think, for ambiguity.

214   Almost every movie you see has sexual situations. When one doesn't, I feel like asking for my money back. No sex, no tension, no conflict, no movie.

The sex doesn't have to be obvious, like four hundred naked extras having an orgy in *Decline and Fall of the Roman Empire.* There is a scene in *Comes a Horseman* in which James Caan and Jane Fonda just look at each other over a rude dinner in her shack. There is more sexual tension in that scene than in the entirety of some R-rated movies. But I doubt that it would even rate a "sexual situations."

So the words used in rating movies do not mean what they mean in other contexts. They are code. The only way to know what they mean is to see the movies.

Humpty Dumpty was almost right. A word means whatever Hollywood wants it to mean.

"I'm Not a Boy, You Know. Never Was"

Mac St. Johns of Thousand Oaks writes:

Gee whiz, Mr. Smith. Now I know how bleak your life must have been when by accident you stumbled into such tension-less, conflict-minus movies as "E.T." "Wilson," "Mr. Smith Goes to Washington," "A Soldier's Story," "Tender Mercies," "Peter Pan," "Cinderella," "Captains Courageous," "Pollyanna," "The Spirit of St. Louis," "The Wizard of Oz," et cetera, et cetera. . . . You poor boy.

First, I may have been exaggerating slightly, exaggeration being allowable to an essayist when he is trying to make a dubious point.

Beyond that, however, I must remind St. Johns, and any others who think all those movies are sexless, that sexual tension permeates our society and is present in almost every situation, however subliminal it may be. I'm not a Freudian scholar, but I think the master would back me up on that.

As for the movies that St. Johns mentions, I can not fairly discuss those I didn't see; but those I did see were certainly loaded with sex.

I haven't seen *E.T.* and *Tender Mercies,* and I can't remember anything of *Captains Courageous* except that Spencer Tracy is out in a rowboat with this little boy in nasty weather; I have the impression that Tracy was dumber than he was courageous.

I saw *Wilson* many years ago and don't remember much about it except that one of Wilson's problems as president was sexual tension. I suspect that every one of our modern presidents has had that problem right up through Carter, except maybe Coolidge, Truman, and Ford. (We know that Carter lusted after women in his heart.)

Mr. Smith Goes to Washington? Surely St. Johns remembers how the sophisticated and cynical Jean Arthur at first laughed at the idealistic young senator, Jimmy Stewart, then fell for him, won over not only by his political integrity and courage but more so by his boyish sexual appeal. Wow! What tension they aroused in us, the audience, until they finally realized they loved (i.e., desired) each other.

A Soldier's Story. I haven't seen the movie, but if it's like the play, its action springs from the unbearable tension in the lives of such men, tightened to the breaking point by the pervasive and ultimate denial—the absence of women. Sexual tension runs through it like a taut E string.

No sex in *Peter Pan?* I haven't seen a modern *Peter Pan,* but I saw Betty Bronson play Peter Pan in the 1920s, when I was but a wee boy, and that lovely, mischievous, elfin young woman became the creature of my earliest sexual fantasies.

Cinderella? Surely I needn't point out that this is the most popular piece of sex symbolism in our literature. The languishing virgin, captive and frustrated, the liberating

prince, libidinous and puissant, the slipper that fits. Good Lord! It is almost too embarrassing to write about!

And *Pollyanna*. Imagine a movie about a bright, healthy, attractive adolescent girl that has no sexual tension in it. But I will say no more about it, lest I be misunderstood.

The Spirit of St. Louis. This was the epic story of every American woman's Lancelot. Lindbergh had no idea of the tensions he released in the disenchanted females of the heartland with his lone thrust through virgin Atlantic skies in that symbolic silver sheath. (And later they sighed when he chose Anne Morrow as his Cinderella, flying her away from imprisonment in her tower of family and wealth.)

The Wizard of Oz. This movie had so much underlying sexual tension it would take a Freud to explain it all. Perhaps I will undertake it someday, for my doctorate.

Just to hint at the depths and complications of it, you have, to begin with, a lion without courage (i.e., impotent); you have a man who is nothing but a scarecrow. (Need I trace the implications of that?) You have a tin man. The very symbol of man's surrender of his humanness to technology.

We have these flawed, frustrated, self-pitying creatures, each less than what he ought to be, singing and dancing their way to see the Wizard in the company of another Pollyanna—a healthy adolescent female, bursting with hope and joy and love, on the threshold of vibrant womanhood. Can you imagine the sexual tensions this whole and buoyant young human being must cause in these inadequate males, loathing the very love they feel for her because they think themselves unworthy of it?

I may have had an advantage in judging *Peter Pan*. Only a few years ago I met Betty Bronson at a cocktail party in the Alexandria Hotel, which had been frequented by the movie crowd in her heyday. When I met her, she was in her late seventies, I would guess, but she still had that playful elfin look. I recognized her at once.

I told her I had seen *Peter Pan* and had loved her ever

since; but I had never thought of her as a boy or as sexless. I had thought of her as a delightful, teasing, enchanting girl.

"So did I," she said. "I'm not a boy, you know. Never was."

I never talked to President Wilson, though. He was before my time.

I've Never Even Seen Her Navel

I was watching a videocassette of *The African Queen* the other day, and it reminded me of how the movies used to handle sex before the present vogue of nudity and heavy breathing.

You may remember that Katharine Hepburn and Humphrey Bogart are thrown together in the riverboat *African Queen* during World War I when Bogart, the captain, rescues her from an African village razed by the Germans.

Miss Hepburn is the sister of Robert Morley, a Methodist missionary who is deranged by the German violence and dies. She is an unmarried woman whose passion has been aroused only by her brother's sermons and by the hymns for which she played the organ in his village church.

In their voyage downriver toward a lake and their showdown with the armed German cruiser *Louisa*, Hepburn and Bogart share many perils and vicissitudes. In her patriotic fervor, she asks Bogart if he can make torpedoes from explosives he has aboard and try to sink the *Louisa*.

Bogart reasonably protests, warning about the dangerous rapids ahead, the German fort they must pass under, and finally, the formidable cruiser with her six-pound gun; but she persuades him to try. Then Bogart gets drunk on gin, says he's changed his mind, and calls Hepburn "a crazy hymn-singing skinny old maid." The next morning, while he watches in the agony of a hangover, she empties his gin bottles in the river and drops them overboard. She refuses to speak to him. He apologizes for his misconduct, saying he

218   can't stand her silence. She tells him it is not his beastly
conduct that has angered her but his change of mind about
sinking the *Louisa*. Once more he caves in.

The propeller shaft is twisted in the rapids. She goads
him into going ashore and repairing it over a fire of charcoal, blacksmithing being one of his many skills.

It is obvious that they are falling in love. Man and
woman thrown together in a struggle for survival always fall
in love. After they pass the German fort, surviving a fusillade of rifle fire, and run the last rapids, they fall jubilantly
into each other's arms, and before you know it, Bogart has
kissed her. Something comes over her. Years of repression
are lifted.

The scene changes to the following morning. We have
seen nothing.

Miss Hepburn is on deck. Bogart is in the previously off-
limits bunk below, feigning sleep. From Hepburn's de-
meanor we know that something significant has happened.
Her face is suffused with a complacent happiness. She is
fresh and buoyant, vibrantly alive. She is the awakened
woman. She makes tea and takes it down to her lover.

That's all there is to it. No flashing of naked backs and
thighs. No tumbling under the sheets. No poignant outcries.
Hepburn standing alone on the deck of the *African Queen*
and reliving the night is among the most erotic perfor-
mances I have ever seen. Imagination fills in the details.

Before their sexual discovery of each other, the two decide they need baths. Bogart goes forward to strip off his
clothes and go overboard; Hepburn undresses in the stern.
We next see her in the water. We see her naked arms and
shoulders. When she tries to get back aboard, she finds that
she can't manage it. The distance between water and gun-
wale is too great. She reaches a naked leg out of the water
and up to the boat, but no luck; she is reduced to asking
Bogart for help.

She says, "Close your eyes." He pulls her up to the boat,
and she emerges from the water modestly attired from neck

to knee in light blue camisole and drawers. That is the closest the movie comes to nudity.

I remember that Hepburn also managed to convey a passionate sexual encounter with Rossano Brazzi in *Summertime* without shedding her garments and hopping into bed with him before our eyes. Once again she is a spinster who is awakened and fulfilled by a heady affair with Brazzi on her brief vacation in Venice. We see nothing specific except that, as I remember, Hepburn loses her shoes.

Like sex, death used to be treated with awe, if not with reverence. It took some time to die. There were tears and last words. "Just break the news to mother," and all that. When I was a small boy, my cousin Donald used to play the player piano at the Saturday night silent movies in the Women's Club in Shafter, a farm town northwest of Bakersfield. When someone died, Donald had time to run through "Nearer My God to Thee" twice.

Nowadays a helicopter lowers from the sky, and a man appears in the doorway with a machine gun and sprays dozens of people on the ground. They fall dead in gouts of blood, and the helicopter soars away.

Then we cut to a scene of two people in bed. Sometimes three.

It is a mark of her quality as an actress that Katharine Hepburn has had a long and glorious career in the movies, from *A Bill of Divorcement* to *On Golden Pond*, and I have never even seen her navel.

IMPROBABLE CONVENIENCES

We Have to Suspend Disbelief

"Suspend disbelief" is a phrase often used by movie critics. It is what a moviegoer must do occasionally to enjoy improbable scenes or stories.

It does not mean that one must suspend disbelief only to enjoy such fantasies as *Star Wars*, but also such theoretically possible situations as that in which the lovers Jack Nicholson and Kathleen Turner, in *Prizzi's Honor*, accept assignments to murder each other.

I see few movies today of any kind that do not require the suspension of disbelief.

Meanwhile, I may be inventing a phrase when I observe that the movies also employ "improbable conveniences" to keep the story moving along.

One of the most common of these occurs when a character is dining out or having a drink and has to leave the table suddenly. Let's say that he is with another woman and his wife walks in. Or his nemesis walks in, looking for him with a gun. Or he sees his quarry leave and has to follow him.

What does he do? Call for his tab, extract money from his wallet and wait for change? Give the waiter his credit card and wait for it to come back with a slip to sign?

Even if he weren't in a desperate hurry, that business would take too long. The audience would grow restless.

221

222   That's when the improbable convenience turns up. What the man does, he reaches into his coat pocket, pulls out a couple of crumpled bills, drops them on the table, and departs.

I am always puzzled that (1) he carries his money loose in his pocket, (2) he always has the exact amount needed to pay the bill and the tip, and (3) he never looks at the bill or counts the money he has withdrawn from his pocket.

Usually the bill hasn't even been delivered yet. He just seems to know that the amount of money he has in his pocket will be exactly right, including tip.

The only alternative to this improbable convenience, or to waiting for the bill and settling with money from his wallet or a credit card, is simply to get up and walk out without paying. But if he were to do that, the audience would scream, "Hey, you forgot to pay!" and the producers would get thousands of letters pointing out this lapse of propriety.

To accept the alternative improbable convenience we have to suspend disbelief.

We see the same phenomenon when our hero leaves a taxicab. He withdraws a couple of loose bills and hands them to the driver without asking for the fare or counting his money. The cabbie always drives on without doing either himself.

One must pay the driver. This is a convention that occurs in every detective-mystery-private-eye novel. Whatever his hurry, the hero never leaves a cab without paying the driver.

In my youth I hoped to become a writer of detective fiction and often read such publications as *Writer's Digest* for tips. Almost every piece I ever read on writing the detective novel said that you must not forget to have your character pay the cabbie.

In a detective novel you will never see a character fail to do this unless he is deliberately stiffing the cabbie and that point is made.

I have an idea that there are editors who know nothing

about the detective novel except that fares must not fail to pay the driver and that they go through manuscripts looking for this malfeasance.

This is really pretty silly. Obviously, if you write that your character "left the cab at Sunset and Selma," you imply that in the act of leaving the cab he paid the fare. Why does every writer of the detective novel have to say that his character paid the fare no matter how big a hurry the reader may be in at this point to get on with the story?

Because if the writer doesn't write that the character paid the fare, he will get 10,000 letters (if the book sells that many copies).

Another improbable convenience is the ignition key left in the parked automobile. In many chase sequences either the hero or the villian, in a big hurry to catch someone or to escape, jumps into a parked car, starts it, and roars off. Many times I have seen fugitives jump into parked *police* cars and roar off.

It is habitual with most people to remove their ignition keys before leaving their cars. We are all too conscious of car thieves to leave our ignition keys in. Most new cars beep if you open the door without first removing the key. I cannot believe that any policeman would walk away from a police car with the ignition keys in it.

Yet in the movies it happens every day.

It is not so much an improbable convenience as an improbable convention of the movies that women emerge from the most uncivilized, harrowing, and physically oppressive ordeals without disarranging their clothes or disturbing their makeup.

My wife and I recently saw the 1950 version of *King Solomon's Mines* with Stewart Granger and Deborah Kerr. For weeks Granger and Miss Kerr trek through the almost impenetrable jungles of unexplored Africa, fighting off snakes, spiders, and rhinoceroses, only to fall into each other's arms in the end. Not only was there no sign that either of them had acquired a trace of body odor, but Miss Kerr hadn't even worked up a sweat.

224   And I don't believe that Stewart Granger paid the bearers.

Fully Clothed Sex

Having been indisposed for a couple of weeks recently, I indulged myself by lying in bed and watching television.

I watched mostly cop series and movies. The cop series are so imitative as to be mere clones of one another, filled with the same clichés.

As for the movies' improbable coincidences, TV has adopted them all. Cop shows could hardly exist unless parking places were always available, pursuing cars always caught up, and keys were always left in ignitions.

There is also the fight, which is perhaps the oldest cliché in movies and has hardly been changed since 1914, when William Farnum and Tom Santschi fought for a full reel in *The Spoilers*.

In these improbable engagements two men beat each other in the face and stomach with their bare fists, smashing furniture, shattering windows, and falling down stairways.

If you have ever seen a serious fistfight, you know that the opponents never last more than a minute or so after the first blows are struck; they are soon too winded and hurt to go on.

In TV shows the hero usually hits the villain first—a good one in the teeth, knocking him sprawling over a table set for dinner, then doubles him up with a fist in the solar plexus, knocking him through a glass door and into a bookcase. In real life, that ought to do it. The hero will have a broken hand and the villain a broken jaw.

But no, the villain pops up, smacking the hero in the jaw with a right, then caving him in with a left to the middle. You wonder that he could have recovered so thoroughly so quickly. Each gains the upper hand at least half a dozen times. Finally, the villain runs, knocking over trash cans to impede the hero, and the chase goes over fences, up stairways, and over rooftops, both men apparently inexhaustible.

I am not suggesting that the classic fistfight be eliminated from our entertainments; it is part of the American myth. There may be time, however, to abort another improbability that has become common, especially in sexy miniseries.

I speak of the love scene in which neither party sheds the most protective and restraining garments. This anomaly, I suspect, is a product of the greater sexual freedom of our times and the ban on nudity in prime-time television.

Back when the Hays Office reigned, the only way to suggest that a scene of sexual passion was taking place was with a shot of a breeze blowing in the curtains of a bedroom window or, as in one daring instance, a train blowing its whistle as it entered a tunnel.

We are refreshingly free of such Victorian rules today. TV may indicate that even unmarried people are making love; but the prohibition of nudity deprives such scenes of a naturalness that some viewers might consider pornographic.

My complaint is that the producers have not yet found a way to reconcile their freedom with their limitations. Consequently, we often see two people falling into bed and engaging, we are meant to assume, in abandoned passion without being suitably unattired.

In the recent miniseries *Napoleon and Josephine*, Napoleon was always falling on Josephine in her bed without bothering to take off his boots, not to mention his pants. I'm not sure that he even took off his sword.

It may be too much to say that Josephine was also fully clothed. She was fully garmented, in the style of the day, but her breasts were always half-exposed, which may account for Napoleon's impetuosity.

My concern is not prurient. I'm not suggesting that prime-time TV go X-rated; but I think they ought not to suggest to the impressionable young that one engages in the ultimate intimacy with nothing but one's shoulders bare.

226   In the Napoleonic series we are led to believe that Josephine couldn't bear Napoleon a child because of a fall she had taken down a stairway. I don't know what the historical truth is, but I suspect that Josephine's infertility was caused by the fact that Napoleon never got his boots off.

LA LA LAND
OF THE NOVEL

Is It the Weather?

"Is it because of the splendid California weather," asks Dan Brennan, "that California has produced only two major novelists—Steinbeck and Jack London?"

For one thing, London was from Oakland, not Southern California, and only Southern California has the kind of weather that is supposed to demoralize and degenerate novelists.

Steinbeck was not a Southern Californian, either. He wrote about the central valleys and coastal towns that he knew so well.

And Steinbeck's best book, according to most critics, was *The Grapes of Wrath*, which was about the misery of impoverished migrants who flocked to the San Joaquin Valley to escape the dust bowls of the Depression.

To be great, it seems, a novelist has to write about the misery of the neighborhood he grew up in and knows. Thus, Sinclair Lewis scored with *Main Street*, a novel about a young wife's attempt to change the philistine life of a small town in the Middle West. *Babbitt*, similarly, was about a businessman's futile attempt to escape the conventions of a small midwestern metropolis. Having grown up in Sauk Centre, Minnesota, Lewis knew the territory.

227

228   "All the major novelists come from the Midwest, South,
        and East," Brennan goes on.

            It might be that the climate house-locks those writ-
            ers for at least half the year. In the South because of
            the heat and in the Midwest because of the freezing
            temperatures. What are you going to do in Minne-
            sota and Nebraska from Nov. 1 through April 30?—
            beget children, drink, hunt, or write. Lots of writers
            do all those things. But above all they turn out
            novels.

        That sounds like Hemingway, an Illinois boy who used
        to hunt and fish in northern Michigan and who spent a lot
        of his adult life womanizing, drinking, hunting, and writing.
            "Look at all the good writers," Brennan says, "novelists
        who came to California from the other climate zones and
        just vanished into Hollywood and the sunny skies and
        beaches."
            William Faulkner comes to mind, and of course F. Scott
        Fitzgerald, both of whom came to Hollywood famous and
        who are said to have languished here.
            "In the Midwest cold months," Brennan argues,
        "there's no temptation to go outdoors. No little voice say-
        ing, go get some beach sunlight or sunbathe on your patio,
        and you can write in the afternoon . . ."
            I get the picture. Imagine a writer who has grown up in
        New York or Chicago and has published a couple of novels
        about life in those cities, to much critical acclaim, working
        through the winter months in his heated flat, getting up
        now and then to look out the window at the snow or have a
        shot of booze or beget a child, but there is nothing to lure
        him outdoors and away from his typewriter. He has to write
        at least until spring comes, the sun melts the snow, and the
        birds begin to sing.
            In Hollywood, what happens to this same writer? He
        sits at his typewriter and puts a piece of paper in and writes
        "Chapter 1." Then he thinks about the moonlight party he

went to the night before at Malibu and the long-legged golden Southern California nymphs he met. The night had been filled with moonlight, music, laughter, and the splash of young bodies in the pool. A refreshing young nymph is no farther away than his telephone. If it isn't a nymph, it's the horse races or a three-martini meeting with his publisher at the Polo Lounge or a story conference with a producer. What novelist can stick to his novel and push on through Chapter 1 when he's been offered $5,000 a page to write a screenplay?

What about the writer who has grown up in Los Angeles? Why can't he write a great novel about growing up in Los Angeles? Because you can't write a serious novel about growing up in La La Land, can you? About surfing and starlit rides in an open convertible and orange trees and balmy weather and scads of healthy beach girls? Where's the tension? Where's the conflict? Where's the misery?

When Lewis and Faulkner and Hemingway were growing up, I'll bet, they went outdoors and chopped wood to work off their frustrations; then they went back indoors and hit the typewriter.

What would a Los Angeles writer do to work off his frustrations? He'd go out on the terrace by the pool and have a gin and tonic and use the poolside phone to call some nymph.

I don't think the booze alone would keep a novelist from being great. After all, three of our Nobel Prize winners —Hemingway, Lewis, and Faulkner—were monumental drinkers. And Steinbeck was no slouch; neither were Fitzgerald, John Cheever, and John O'Hara.

I remember when I was in high school my English teacher told us that the great writers came from northern climes, for very much the same reasons cited by Brennan.

I figured right then that I would never be a great writer because I can't bear cold weather; but then I began to wonder about some of the great books written by Mediterraneans, including the Bible. Certainly men who wrote the Bible

230   never saw much snow, and I imagine there were dancing
girls and wine and other temptations even in those days.

If Matthew, Mark, Luke, and John could do it, why
can't I?

Let's see—where was I?

"It was the end of summer . . ."

Oh, well, maybe I'll just go out and try the pool and
have a beer.

They Followed the Sun

Because life is too easy here, Southern California may never
produce a major novelist, but its yield of letter writers is
abundant.

Dan Brennan's notion that our blissful climate has undone all but two major novelists has at least stirred several
Angelenos from their lethargy to their typewriters.

Gladwin Hill, who was long a correspondent for *The
New York Times* but now lives here in easy retirement just
below the Hollywood sign, says the rationale for Southern
California's low incidence of major novelists is "quite simple." He writes:

> As you know, California is composed largely of peo-
> ple from somewhere else, who migrated here for one
> of two reasons: escapism or the entrepreneurial
> spirit, the yen for adventure or novelty.
>
> Neither sort is essentially the novel-writing type.
> Novel-writing . . . is possibly the poorest-paid oc-
> cupation there is. . . . Your escapist Californian is
> probably going to be diverted into some form of
> cultism and lose interest in completing his/her
> novel. . . . He's going to go into real estate or in-
> vent something or go into quiche franchising. . . .
>
> The weather indeed *attracts* people to California.
> But the crucial point is the *sort* of people who are

attracted by weather, and California's numerous other attractions.

Hill certainly has a point. In analyzing the effect of migration on any city we have to consider the *kind* of people who have migrated to it.

I have always believed that one reason for the vitality, the freshness of spirit, and the buoyancy of America was the *kind* of people who came here from other continents. They were not the same as those they left behind. They were daring; they had energy; they had the desire to be free, to leave the past behind, to challenge the unknown; they followed the sun.

The people who migrate to Los Angeles are still following the sun, but they are not as tough as the Europeans who turned up at Ellis Island with their strange names and their bundles, reckless of danger, undismayed by hardship, determined to strive and succeed.

Perhaps the Asians and Latinos who are streaming into Los Angeles today are of that kind, burning with entrepreneurial zeal and a hunger for freedom, but most Americans who migrate here from other quarters of the nation are drawn by visions of balmy winters, warm swimming pools, easy morals, casual clothing, and laid-back life-styles. To begin with, they are tired. They want warmth and comfort, not challenge.

Of course there are the young who migrate here by the thousands. They may not be tired, but they come here, too, for the easiness, for visions of sugarplums, of instant stardom and riches. They come here for identity, and they are lost. One of them, someday, may write a major novel.

Howard Decker of North Hollywood calls Brennan's idea "specious," and asks "What about Richard Henry Dana?"

Dana was the Harvard man who sailed to California as an ordinary seaman and wrote *Two Years Before the Mast.* It was a popular and influential book, but it was not a novel.

Decker also nominates Raymond Chandler, "who is

LaLaLand

232   considered a major novelist in more civilized climes, like Europe, and especially Great Britain."

I must have read each of Chandler's four major novels at least three times, and while they enjoyed a wide popular success as detective stories, they were indeed serious novels in depicting the efforts of a modern knight-errant to right wrongs and vanquish evil against a Southern California landscape that reeked of greed, corruption, the exploitation of the innocent, and old orchids.

Still, Chandler was not untouched by the degenerative afflictions that Southern California visits on good writers. He finally drank himself to death in his La Jolla apartment.

"Faulkner . . . wrote some of his best stuff here (in Hollywood)," Decker goes on. "So did Fitzgerald. What about Cain and Nathanael West? How about Lillian Hellman? She prospered in Hollywood, and I can't believe that this fact didn't help 'produce' her work. A novelist uses every ounce of his/her life's blood and experiences. . . ."

Faulkner wrote movies here and drank. I don't think any of his novels has a California background. Fitzgerald was working on a Hollywood novel, *The Last Tycoon*, when he died in the Hollywood apartment of his friend, Sheila Graham.

James M. Cain wrote *Serenade* and *Mildred Pierce*, both set in Southern California. Does anyone still read them? Budd Schulberg wrote the excellent *What Makes Sammy Run?* about an opportunistic film executive.

Nathanael West? He wrote one highly praised short novel about the destruction of the innocents in Hollywood.

"The smog didn't hurt Aldous Huxley's muse," writes novelist Marianne Ruuth. "Christopher Isherwood thrived next to the Pacific Ocean. . . ."

She also mentions Ray Bradbury, Henry Miller, and others. Huxley and Isherwood, it seems to me, wound up in left field courting the occult. Bradbury will outlast them both, but his greatest novel was about Mars, not Los Angeles. (Maybe there isn't that much difference.)

Contrary to Hill's law, Jacqueline Briskin, Judith

Krantz, Harold Robbins, and Sidney Sheldon have all got rich writing novels but have not won critical acclaim.

As Ruuth says, Los Angeles has produced many good writers. But I'm not sure that any is a "major American novelist."

I do know that Gladwin Hill and Robert Decker are never going to make it. Not if they go on writing *"his/her."*

Don't Rankle a Philosophy Major

In examining novelist Dan Brenner's notion that Southern California's bland climate and sensual temptations keep great novelists from writing great works here, I did not mean to undertake a serious study of the Los Angeles novel. I am neither a novelist (yet) nor a literary critic nor even a serious student of the form.

However, for suggesting that there might be some truth in Brenner's thesis, I have been called everything from blasphemous to sexist, both of which I well may be. I was more interested in the implied slur on the Los Angeles scene than I was in a comparative analysis of the Los Angeles novel.

I'm sure the "great American novel" is an ideal that has never been achieved, and never will be.

As I said, Cain, West, Schulberg, and Chandler have written gutsy and eloquent novels with a Los Angeles scene, and Fitzgerald had six chapters of one going when he died.

Of course, I have received protests from champions of every other novelist who ever passed through Los Angeles on a Greyhound bus and some who didn't even get that close.

Tracy Cummings, a philosophy major at UC San Diego, calls me a sexist for not naming any women among those whom I dismissed as not having written the "great American novel" about Los Angeles and names such women writ-

234   ers as Emily Dickinson, Willa Cather, and Emily Brontë—none of whom, so far as I know, ever breathed a breath of L.A. smog.

"Let me warn you," she says, "it is not wise to rankle a philosophy major or a philosopher, since we and they can tear you to shreds with logic."

Ms. Cummings also deplores my description of Southern California women as "long-legged, golden . . . young nymphs" and points out, quite correctly, that not all Southern California women have long legs and suntans.

"None are nymphs," she insists, "unless you prefer to refer to women in somewhat poetic terms that make us seem like magical creatures with nothing better to do than have fun. . . ."

Don Weddle of Buena Park argues that the malaise, frustration, and conflict that underlie great novels are to be found here in Lotus Land. He writes:

> I doubt that even you could be such an astute observer of life "if you had not experienced at least a little bit of tension, rage, anxiety, depression, unhappy marriage, unfulfilled dreams, impotency, problems with children, chronic physical illness, addictions, competition for employment, mid-life crisis, fears, child and spousal abuse—who could be happy without one or another of them now and then?

Well, I can't plead guilty to *all* those afflictions, but I *have* experienced mid-life crisis.

Weddle also points out, in reference to the first line of my own unfinished novel, that there is no such thing here as "the end of summer."

Hilda Reach reminds me that the Nobel novelist Thomas Mann lived in Pacific Palisades from 1941 to 1952.

"I was his secretary for almost 10 of those 12 years, and (he) managed to stay out of the pools and away from the booze and the beach girls."

Mann won the Nobel Prize in 1929, when he lived in   **235**
Germany. He came to the United States as a refugee from
the Nazis in 1939, and in the years that he lived here he
continued to write in German and about Europe. I might
have liked his books better if he had written more about
booze and beach girls.

"You mention no female scribes in Lotus Land," writes
Corinne Greiner of Iowa City, Iowa. "Have Joan Didion,
Wanda Coleman and their peers written off into the sun-
set?"

Ms. Greiner says she is "normally" a Californian, but in
the past year she has experienced

> every glory of life in the Midwest—dragon-sized
> mosquitoes, humidity that transformed me into an
> oozing blob; hayfever which made my nose resemble
> Bozo's; seventy-below temperatures; winds so fierce
> they literally knocked me over. According to Mr.
> Brennan and yourself I should be a Nobel laureate
> by now. . . .

Ms. Greiner notes that she has had several short stories
published, "perhaps because I've been enlightened by
Iowa's lack of sunsets and orange trees, [but]I find it difficult to believe that last summer's allergies and this winter's
frostbite will turn me into Jane Austen. . . ."

Carl Karnig Mahakian of Burbank describes William
Saroyan, quoting Donald Heiney, professor of English at
UC Irvine, as "one of the most American of 20th Century
writers."

But Saroyan's native territory was *Fresno*. He knew
nothing of Los Angeles and its beach girls.

"What about Joseph Wambaugh?" asks Arline Stone.
"A *Times* reviewer said that if Southern California had produced a better author he couldn't think of who it was."

Neither can I. Wambaugh may be as good as any we've
had. His books, even more than Chandler's, reflect the utter
corruption of character in the Los Angeles environment,

236   but his cop heroes, like Chandler's Marlowe, are sustained by some untouchable core of integrity.

As long as we're trying to be thorough, I ought to mention Horace McCoy, whose 1935 novel *They Shoot Horses, Don't They?* used the dreary marathon dances of the Depression as a metaphor for the despair of life in Los Angeles, and Alison Lurie, whose satirical *The Nowhere City* gave us one of our most lasting epithets.

Now, back to my own novel, which, I promise you, will be filled with women who seem like magical creatures with nothing better to do than have fun.

I'm shooting for a miniseries.

I DON'T LIKE VEGETABLES

"Eat Your Asparagus"

"You aren't eating your asparagus," my wife said the other evening at dinner.

"I don't like vegetables," I said.

She put down her fork and looked at me as if I had just confessed that I was a serial killer.

"You don't like vegetables?" she said incredulously.

"I have never liked vegetables." As long as I had come out with it, I thought, I might as well go all the way.

"How come," she said evenly, "you have never mentioned it in forty years?"

"Closer to forty-seven," I said.

"How about artichokes?" she said. "Don't you like artichokes?"

Of all vegetables, I hate artichokes the most. I confessed it. In the first place, I pointed out, eating them is an ordeal. One must peel the leaves off one by one, making sure not to get pricked on a fingertip by the spines, then dip them in the melted butter and *scrape* them off the leaf by pulling them through one's clenched teeth. In this process one creates an enormous heap of discarded leaves that must either be dropped onto one's plate or into a bowl especially provided for that purpose.

237

"It's tedious," I pointed out. "Also, there's something primitive and ritualistic about it."

And then, when you get down to the heart, you have to gouge out all those terrible little spears, which, I have no doubt, it would be fatal to consume.

I knew I was wounding her. The artichoke is one of her favorite vegetables, and she loves them all. She would be very happy as a vegetarian.

"Well," she said. "I can't believe it. That in all these years you've never said anything."

"It just never came up," I explained weakly.

"I thought you liked beans."

I admitted, with enthusiasm, that I liked beans; especially refried beans.

"How about potatoes? Don't you like potatoes?"

I could also say that I liked potatoes. Especially hash brown, or baked with butter.

"What about green beans?"

Why did I start being honest? "I hate green beans," I confessed.

"Why didn't you ever say so?"

"Well, I knew that you liked them. I didn't want to deprive you of that pleasure."

She wasn't finished yet. "What about brussels sprouts?"

Brussels sprouts! The very thought of brussels sprouts makes me ill. When I was a small boy, my mother was always serving brussels sprouts, and I despised them.

I had an Aunt Betty who sometimes ate at our house, and when she did, she gallantly ate all the brussels sprouts on my plate. My mother pretended not to notice. I always loved my Aunt Betty for that.

My mother also insisted that I eat my broccoli, which was just coming into fashion. Our relationship was exactly illustrated by that famous *New Yorker* cartoon of the mother assuring her little girl, "It's broccoli, dear," and the little girl replying, "I say it's spinach, and I say the hell with it."

Spinach, by the way, is the worst of all. It reminds me of seaweed.

If anything is worse than brussels sprouts and spinach, it's turnips. How I hate turnips! I can hardly believe that whole nations in Eastern Europe have survived on turnips and potatoes.

"How about eggplant?" she said.

I was afraid she was going to ask about eggplant. She loves eggplant. She has the notion that eggplant can be disguised to substitute for meat and is always cooking up something like eggplant parmigiana, in which eggplant is fried or baked with cheese.

You can't fool me with eggplant. It is not veal, and no amount of spices and parmigiana will make it taste like veal.

"Don't you like peas?"

For one thing, I have always resented the amount of work that goes into preparing peas for the table. I remember too well my hours of drudgery in the kitchen after school, shelling peas for dinner. Then, adding nausea to tedium, I had to eat them.

"I've just never liked your going to all that trouble," I said.

She said, "You like jicama, don't you?"

"What's jicama?" I asked suspiciously.

She explained that jicama is a white stalky vegetable, about as crisp as a carrot but juicy and slightly sweet.

"You're always eating it at cocktail parties," she said, "with your wine."

"Oh, that," I said. I do eat it at cocktail parties, I explained, because to sustain life at those rituals one must eat whatever is offered, and it is either jicama or zucchini or mushrooms, which are worse.

"How about tomatoes?"

"Tomatoes are a fruit, not a vegetable," I pointed out. "Anyway, I don't like them except in soup or salsa."

I knew I was probably about to lose my cook, but I couldn't stop.

"I also don't like squash," I said, knowing it was one of

240   her favorites, "and just as a warning, don't ever serve me
rhubarb."

She said, "Eat your asparagus."

"We Have a Gender-Defining Syndrome Here"

My disclosure that I have never liked vegetables has
brought me both cheers and poisoned arrows.

Many readers doubted that my wife could have remained ignorant of this frailty for forty-seven years. They
simply do not understand that I am rather a private person,
not given to self-revelation.

Not surprisingly, more men applauded me than women.
Is it possible that women have more of an affinity for vegetables than men? It seems to be true, at least, in the Charlton Heston household. He writes:

> Your piece on vegetables struck a resonant chord.
> I don't like them much either. I think we have a
> gender-defining syndrome here. Men tend to dislike
> vegetables, women tend to like them. My wife's re-
> action to your column was succinct: "It's stupid not
> to like vegetables!" I myself confess to an accommo-
> dation of spinach and cucumbers, but we great hu-
> manitarians are noted for our tolerance.

Seymour Holtzman of Arcadia writes that his household
is similarly split:

> For years I concealed this shortcoming of mine by
> waiting until my wife turned her head away at the
> table or got up to serve, and very quickly I would
> transfer the vegetables on my plate onto her plate.

I wonder if Holtzman doesn't underestimate his wife.
My guess is that she was playing along with his trick to get
more than her share.

Joy Garcia of Sherman Oaks recalls that as a child she
employed an even more desperate deceit to avoid eating
string beans. "My mother served them very overcooked and
consequently very gray. I had to stay at the dinner table
until they were consumed. Many a lonely evening was spent
in this manner. After a while I started putting them in my
pockets. Then, when released, I'd run outside and give them
to the dog."

Inevitably, she was caught. She forgot to empty her
pockets, and her mother found the string beans when she
washed her jeans.

"I still hate string beans, brussels sprouts, and (the
worst) eggplant."

"I too loathe vegetables," writes Bill Gordon of Fullerton. "Vegetable soup is palatable as long as it is cooked to
the point that the vegetables are tasteless and in small
enough pieces to be swallowed whole.

"I am disappointed to know that you have wimped out
all of these years and have actually eaten that disgusting
stuff to please your wife."

Several people have written to say that my wife evidently doesn't know how to prepare artichokes or I
wouldn't find them so disagreeable. I'm not about to question my wife's cooking just to exonerate an inedible vegetable.

The other night she served artichokes again, but first
cut off the swordlike tips that antagonize me so much. It
was a good try, but it didn't change the taste any.

I am also told that the hateful "choke," the furry, spiny
part that guards the heart from human access, may be easily
removed with a knife.

"Those terrible little spears you mention," writes Wil-

242   liam Robb of Orcutt, "make up the choke. It can be removed quite easily."

Robb is an expert on vegetables, being an agriculture biologist with the Office of the Agricultural Commissioner in Santa Barbara. He says that those things I call leaves, with the sword points, are not leaves. "What you eat are the *bracts*. The spines you refer to are called thorns."

I can't say that replacing the word *leaves* with *bracts* and *spines* with *thorns* makes the artichoke any more palatable.

Ruth Brower also advises me on getting rid of the choke. "With a small, sharp knife and a skillful movement all the little spears can be removed very easily, in one piece. (And it's fun to do it.)"

Fun? How much do you want to bet I could do it without drawing blood?

Stan Leland agrees with me but warns against the "cunning" of the cook.

"Only last night I was served a delicious cream soup, which I relished, but which, I was informed after my second bowl, had as its basic ingredient, br. . . . i. I can't get myself to write the word, let alone eat the stuff."

I'm afraid Leland's belated reaction betrays a prejudice that I may well share. I think that's why I keep trying.

Carl H. Wennerberg of Valley Center tells me there is good scientific evidence for eschewing spinach.

"Dr. Roger Truesdale, founder of the laboratories of the same name and a former professor of chemistry at Pomona College, did a very important study that demonstrated that spinach ties up the calcium in a person's system."

Inevitably I heard from vegetarians who believe it is inhumane to eat other animals and that only through vegetarianism will the race become benign and loving.

This philosophy was expressed with his usual felicity by the great humanist Henry David Thoreau: "I have no doubt that it is part of the destiny of the human race, in its gradual improvement, to leave off eating animals, as surely as the savage tribes have left off eating each other when they

come in contact with the more civilized." (By the way, it
was those more civilized tribes that gave the Tahitians tuberculosis and syphilis.)

And George Bernard Shaw observed: "Ferocity is still characteristic of bulls and other vegetarians."

On the other hand, we dined with friends at Spago the other night, and I had angel-hair pasta with broccoli, goat cheese, and thyme.

It was divine.

DOOMSDAY

A Bang or a Whimper?

For years I have been collecting a file on the end of the world. I call it my Doomsday file.

I have reported on this file before, but I feel an update is called for. It may be that I have been wasting my time. The latest scientific fad is not predicting the end of the world but the end of the universe.

That really leaves us nowhere to go. I had little hope that we could escape our planet and take refuge on another one before ours is burned to a cinder, knocked out of orbit by an errant comet, or turned to ice by the death of the sun. But at least there was a chance, if we were clever enough, that somewhere else in the universe we could find a home.

Realistically, I think we are doomed to live and die on our planet, but I suspect that in the time of Copernicus I would have argued that the sun revolved around the earth and that in the time of Calvin Coolidge I would have argued that men would never reach the moon.

One of my Doomsday theories is contraindicated. It is logically pointed out that the earth will not be reduced to ice by the sun's extinction because long before it goes out the sun will expand into a bloated mass that will boil the oceans and burn the earth to a crisp.

So that's one worry eliminated, if you don't care for ice.

246   It will be a long time before the sun collapses and then expands; but we are told that it's shrinking right now at the rate of four or five miles a year, so it's going to go out sooner or later.

We also have to worry about the next arrival of a rampant comet of the kind that hit the earth 60 million years ago, wiping out the dinosaurs, who were blameless. Astronomers are now convinced that these visitors have been impacting the earth with regularity and that the next one is due in about 14 million years.

That's not the day after tomorrow, but still, if one is thinking about human survival, it isn't long.

Then we have the greenhouse effect. Scientists are worried that the continued release of industrial gases into the atmosphere will not only destroy the ozone layer that protects us from excessive ultraviolet rays but also raise the earth's temperature enough to melt the polar ice caps and flood our coastal cities—such as New York, San Francisco, and Los Angeles.

That might not do away with us altogether, but it would certainly change our lifestyle. Imagine life without the Big Apple, Frisco, or, what the heck, Hollywood.

Meanwhile, the earth's spin is slowing. Scientists estimate that 500 million years from now a day will last about 31 hours. Eventually, if this keeps up, the earth will stop, presenting only one side to the sun, so that we will either burn up or freeze.

If we are really crazy enough to have an atomic war, scientists warn, we will create a nuclear winter—an umbrella of atmospheric dust and debris that will shut out the sun and destroy whatever life has been left.

If we avoid atomic war, we will probably breed ourselves into extinction. A reader, David Simmons, calculates that if we keep doubling our population every 37 years, as we are doing now, in only 230 years the entire land surface of the earth will have the population density of Manhattan. Imagine how hard it would be to get a cab, much more get into a decent restaurant.

Now, according to a story in *Discover* magazine, scientists can't decide whether the universe will collapse and end in a black crunch or whether it will go on expanding, as it has been doing ever since the Big Bang, into eternity.

Either way, you wouldn't want to take a long-term position in it.

If the universe collapses, increasing radiation will turn it bright as the sun, stars will die, and the whole ball of wax will vanish in one big black hole.

Says Tony Rothman, author of the article, "A civilization may bury itself underground to avoid the increasingly severe microwave burn, but there's no escape. . . . No deus ex machina will save (us) from cosmic incineration."

On the other hand, the universe may not collapse. It may go on expanding into eternity. But there is not a great deal to look forward to in that, either.

In 100 trillion years all the stars will have burned out. Meanwhile, vagabond stars will have pulled the planets out of orbit. Rothman sees a time when "the earth would probably be wandering lifeless among dead stars and the sun's corpse would be orbiting in the galactic halo. . . ."

I have greatly simplified the theories, but any way you look at it, the future is not promising.

Considering our options, it seems to me that the best thing we can do is to keep on as we are, pour our gases into the atmosphere, destroy the ozone layer, raise the temperature, and turn the planet over to flood and ice.

Wouldn't that be better than ending up in a black hole?

Robert Frost decided, in a memorable poem, that between fire and ice, he thought that ice would suffice.

T. S. Eliot gave us all pause when he questioned whether the world would end with a bang or a whimper.

I suggest that we just go on doing the best we can and see what happens.

248

Who's Afraid of the Greenhouse Effect?

I was startled the other day by the following headline, which a reader had clipped and sent to me from our Orange County edition: "Deportation Day Looming for Man."

His immediate reaction on reading this, wrote John W. Marienthal of Anaheim, was alarm. He said, "I figured the human race was being shipped to the moon!"

As it turned out, the man referred to was not mankind but a man the immigration service was trying to deport.

One may wonder, though, if such a headline might someday mean what it seems to mean.

Doomsday watching isn't as simple as it was when we knew that the world was going to come to an end but the end was billions of years off; so why worry?

What we Doomsday watchers hope to see are signs of some catastrophe that will intercede in this scenario, bumbling onstage like some character the playwright hadn't conceived of and preempting the final act.

Except for their entertainment value, I have never paid much attention to the sidewalk prophets—James Thurber's "get ready men"—who warn us to prepare for Judgment Day, when the angels of the Lord will destroy the earth, and only the chosen, who have gathered on the appointed plain, will be lifted into heaven.

I never used to worry much either about Armageddon, that final battle between the forces of good and evil, since I grew up counting on the Atlantic Ocean to separate the two and an Armageddon seemed logistically impossible.

Now, of course, we know that Armageddon may be only a push button away and that that final battle indeed may be fought, though neither the good nor the evil will survive it to answer roll call.

What concerns me is that we have grown indifferent to our drift toward self-destruction because both science and religion have persuaded us that the world is doomed, anyway. So why not write our own script and go out with a bang—the way we came in?

The goal of Doomsday watching is to offset the dark prospects with the bright, to nourish hope.

The last time I toted things up, I noted the then-popular theory that the growing amount of carbon dioxide in the atmosphere was creating a "greenhouse effect" that would raise the temperature, melting the polar ice caps, raising the sea level, and flooding the earth.

But wait. It has been found, according to an item in the *National Review,* that "termites, digesting vegetable matter, release twice as much carbon dioxide into the atmosphere as all of man's puny efforts put together."

The opportunity this bit of knowledge offers is exciting. No need to get rid of ourselves. Simply get rid of our termites. It's not a job for the Pentagon or the Kremlin but for Western Exterminator. (They're in the Yellow Pages.)

As if that weren't good news enough, we have even more recently been assured by a U.S. Department of Agriculture physicist that the greenhouse effect is actually a good thing. Even if the carbon dioxide were to double or triple, he says, the increase in heat would be harmless, but it would be enough to increase the world's agricultural production 20–30 percent.

So who's afraid of the greenhouse effect? All it means is bigger tomatoes.

On the other hand, marine biologist Joel Hedgpeth, founder and president of the Society for the Prevention of Progress, says that man is destroying his paradise with pesticides, antibiotics, detergents, and atomic energy and his doom is only decades away.

On the other hand, Herman Kahn, who can talk Doomsday with the gloomiest of us, recently said right here in Los Angeles that our technology is taming pollution and new and traditional values have synthesized to effect a cure for the malaise of the last twenty years. (He admitted,

250   though, that he had his briefcase filled with "disaster scenarios.")

According to AP, a bolt of lightning recently struck a group of Indians during a dance ceremony at an archaeological site in the Puye Cliffs area near Santa Clara Pueblo, New Mexico, killing two persons.

When a bolt of lightning kills a person, it is always taken as a sign, but so far it hasn't happened frequently enough to mean that someone is growing impatient with us as a species; he's merely zapping individuals, willy-nilly.

According to another AP story, out of New York, lightning strikes only about one person in a million every year, which isn't enough to worry about, unless you happen to be a one-in-a-million sort of person.

But gloom is hard to chase. John J. Kassenbrock of Laguna Hills recently sent me this paragraph from an editorial:

> It is a gloomy moment in the history of our country. The domestic economic situation is in chaos. Our dollar is weak throughout the world. Prices are so high as to be utterly impossible. The political caldron seethes and bubbles with uncertainty. Russia hangs, as usual, like a cloud, dark and silent, upon the horizon. Of our troubles, no man can see the end.

That was in *Harper's* magazine in 1930.

L.A. SONG

"It's Where You See the Movie Stars"

Henry Tobias, the prolific and perennial Hollywood song-writer, writes to give me his professional opinion why Los Angeles has never produced an "official" song.

I have considered this question several times over the years and always come up with a blank, though numerous songwriters have sent me their Los Angeles songs, either in sheet music or on tape.

None of them seem to have made it into the public consciousness.

Los Angeles still has no song that touches the nostalgic heart strings like "New York, New York," "I Left My Heart in San Francisco," and "Chicago, Chicago."

One obvious reason, as I have pointed out, is that Los Angeles doesn't have a good meter for music. You can't sing "Los Angeles, Los Angeles."

Like *orange*, it doesn't rhyme with anything, either; but then neither does San Francisco, New York, or Chicago. (Well, *York* rhymes with *pork*.)

Maybe Los Angeles doesn't inspire a great song for the same reason it doesn't inspire a great novel. It's just too debilitating out there by the pool in the sun. No one has the *energy* to write a great song.

251

252   Tobias thinks it's because the city tried sponsoring a contest for a Los Angeles song, hoping to produce one that could become the city's "official" song by proclamation.

That contest ended quietly some years ago when the city, deluged by tons of unsingable songs, bored by poetic invocations of palm trees, sunsets, snow-covered mountains, surf, moonlight, suntanned girls, orange trees, and even freeways, decided to abandon the project and let nature take its course.

What causes Tobias to raise the subject again is an invitation he has received from Nashville, Tennessee, to submit a song in a contest for "an official Nashville song."

The letter comes from Maggie Cavender, executive director of the Nashville Songwriters Association International, and Kathy Hyland, regional director of the Nashville Songwriters Guild, at the request of Nashville's mayor, Richard Fulton.

"The mayor has asked us to let you know that Nashville is looking for a song!" it says. "New York, Chicago, Los Angeles, San Francisco and many other cities are highly visible through the songs they have adopted as official themes. . . ." (I don't know what Los Angeles song she's talking about.)

It adds that the song "should be adaptable to all musical styles," and that it will be performed by the Nashville Symphony Orchestra at the Summer Lights Festival, June 1.

That implies that the mayor and his people have no doubt that an "official" song will be forthcoming.

The contest is limited to writers who have had a top-ten song in a recognized national trade publication, which would eliminate the kind of amateurs who cluttered the Los Angeles competition.

Tobias says he is gratified to be invited to compete, and certainly he and his brothers, Harry and Charles, have had many hits, including "Miss You," "Sweet and Lovely," "Sail Along, Silv'ry Moon," "I'm Sorry Dear," and "If I Knew Then."

Then why is Henry Tobias rejecting this invitation?

"I think you are wasting your time," he wrote to Nashville, "asking any writer *not from Nashville* to compete.

I wouldn't even try to compete in writing an L.A. song, which I was asked to do, for the following reason: I believe that official songs should be decided by the *public*, and not by competition or publicity or political connections.

Take any well-known official city song. New York had "East Side, West Side" for many years because the public wanted it. Then when Frank Sinatra came along with his "New York, New York" the public loved it and it became an *unofficial* New York City song. . . .

He noted that Los Angeles had asked many well-known writers to write a city song, without success.

Then Randy Newman came along with some political connections at City Hall and got an official blessing from the Olympics to use his song, which incidentally . . . was very bad and instead of praising L.A. it knocked it and was not accepted by the public.

"You can take a horse to the well but you can't make him drink," Tobias concludes.

I don't recall that Randy Newman's song had any friends at city hall, but it was a big hit during the Olympic Games because of its repetition on television. I predicted at the time, though, that it would not last, because it was unsingable and unmemorable. I don't think I have ever heard anyone humming it, and as far as I know, it is quite forgotten.

Meanwhile, since I last mentioned this problem, I have received numerous original songs such as "They Call It

254   L.A.," words and music by Douglas Simmonds, a fragment of which goes like this:

> They call it L.A., Los Angeles, the city of the Angels,
> The only place I want to stay. . . .
> It's where you see the movie stars,
> the beautiful girls, the fancy cars.
> It's a show place, a get up and go place,
> and people greet you with a smile,
> the city dazzles you with style,
> a fun place, a play in the sun place,
> they call it L.A. . . .

Here's a bit of "You Can't Stay Away from L.A." words and music by Jack Quigley:

> It's a pot full of promise filled with sunshine and wine
> Spotlights and Hollywood and Vine,
> Palm trees and light breezes,
> Freeways and tight squeezes
> . . . Angel, you're all mine!

> Bring me my sunglasses, please, and a beer. . . .

But Does It Sing?

Pierce Rollins takes exception to my notion that the name *Los Angeles* does not lend itself to musical meter. He argues that I am trying to fit Los Angeles into the wrong songs.

He points out that Los Angeles fits easily into "America the Beautiful," which begins "Oh, beautiful for spacious skies." He asks, Why not "Los Angeles, Los Angeles, a city great and proud . . . ?"

Okay. That sings, but I don't think a song about Los

Angeles ought to attempt the grandeur of "America the Beautiful."

He also suggests "God bless Los Angeles, city we love," to the tune of "God Bless America."

Again, I think it is a bit presumptuous for Los Angeles to ask God's blessing, considering our wayward ways.

If we squeeze the pronunciation a bit, he suggests, making it "Los Anj-less," we can sing it to "Columbia, the Gem of the Ocean"—"Los Anj-less, a gem of a city."

The closest Rollins comes to inspiration is in his suggestion that we can sing "It's Los Angeles, the city that we call L.A.," to the tune of "On the Atchison, Topeka and the Santa Fe."

Somehow I don't think that fitting the name *Los Angeles* to religious or patriotic anthems will capture the special ambience of this city. Also, any lyrics that suggest pride are out. We can hardly take pride in our weather, which just is. And everything else we are comes from our weather.

Rather than expressing pride, a song seeking to evoke Los Angeles ought to mention those phenomena that make life special here: the smog, the polluted seashore, the littered sidewalks, the crowded freeways, the street crime, the high school dropout rate, the homeless, the sleaze, the decay, the high cost of housing, our failure to support libraries, our failing emergency hospital system, the general apathy.

On the other hand, we should be forgiven for singing of our relatively honest government, our uncorrupt police department, our splendid fire department, our excellent universities, our friendliness, our racial tolerance, our palms and jacarandas, our flowers, our sexual and religious freedom, our world championship baseball and basketball teams, our theater, our restaurants (which even Herb Caen admits are better than San Francisco's), our sunshine, our good cheer, our outdoor life, and the annual UCLA-USC football game.

Rollins concludes,

256   I, too, take my hat off to Billy Barnes's "L.A. Is,"
but as another writer of special material I am convinced it is possible for a "Los Angeles" song to be
written that is easily a match for "Moon over
Miami" or "I Left My Heart in San Francisco." I
may even take a shot at it.

If any song about Los Angeles ever catches on, in the
way that "New York, New York" has caught on as a theme
song for that city, I am sure it will use the name "L.A."
rather than "Los Angeles,' which seems to fit only into
hymns and anthems and which evokes a saintliness that we
Angelenos do not deserve.
      I can't write music, but I'll try some lyrics. How about:

      L.A., I love your sleaze,
      Your palms and jacaranda trees;
      I love your Thai and Chinese food,
      Your women, slim and seminude;
      I love your outdoor barbecues,
      Your California wines and booze,
      Your weather, warm and sunny;
      Your people, laid back, funny;
      I love your Trojans and your Bruins,
      Your warm Decembers, cloudy Junes;
      I love your kitsch, your con and hustle,
      Your fads, your health, your muscle;
      I love your freedom and your show;
      L.A. you turn me on, you make me glow.

I wouldn't be surprised if that could be sung to something by Mozart, or maybe Cole Porter.